Careers in Focus

GERIATRIC CARE

THIRD EDITION

Ferguson
An imprint of Infobase Publishing

Careers in Focus: Geriatric, Third Edition

Ferguson
An imprint of Infobase Publishing
132 West 31st Street
New York NY 10001

Library of Congress Cataloging-in-Publication Data

Careers in focus. Geriatric care. — 3rd ed.
    p. ; cm.
  Other title: Geriatric care
  Includes bibliographical references and index.
  ISBN-13: 978-0-8160-8025-0 (hardcover : alk. paper)
  ISBN-10: 0-8160-8025-9 (hardcover : alk. paper) 1. Geriatrics—Vocational
guidance. I. Ferguson Publishing. II. Title: Geriatric care.
  [DNLM: 1. Geriatrics. 2. Career Choice. 3. Vocational Guidance. WT 21]
  RC952.5.C34 2010
  618.97'023—dc22
                                    2010025279

Ferguson books are available at special discounts when purchased in bulk quanti- ties for businesses, associations, institutions, or sales promotions. Please call our Special Sales Department in New York at (212) 967-8800 or (800) 322-8755.

You can find Ferguson on the World Wide Web at http://www.fergpubco.com

Text design by David Strelecky
Composition by Mary Susan Ryan-Flynn
Cover printed by Art Print Company, Taylor, PA
Book printed and bound by Maple Press, PA
Date printed: December 2010
Printed in the United States of America

10 9 8 7 6 5 4 3 2 1

This book is printed on acid-free paper.

All links and Web addresses were checked and verified to be correct at the time of publication. Because of the dynamic nature of the Web, some addresses and links may have changed since publication and may no longer be valid.

Table of Contents

Introduction

The term *geriatric care* refers to a career field in which professionals work with elderly people. In some cases, these professionals (such as adult day care coordinators and geriatric care managers) have jobs that allow them to focus on providing services solely to elderly clients. In other cases geriatric care professionals (such as creative arts therapists and financial planners) have jobs that allow them to work with a variety of clients, and they may choose to work with or simply find that a large number of their clients are senior citizens.

When you are 15 or 16 years old, age 26 might sound unbearably old to you. When you are 30, age 50 might seem "elderly." So when does "old" officially begin? For the purposes of this book, we use age terms in the same way the federal government does. That is, broad terms such as *elderly, geriatric,* and *senior citizen* refer to a large and diverse group of people age 65 and older.

Geriatric care careers will be of particular importance in the coming years. One reason for this is that the senior population is large and growing every year. The Administration on Aging reported that approximately 35 million Americans were age 65 or older in 2000, and it expects this number to more than double to 71.5 million by 2030 as the population grows and people continue to live longer. In the next several years, the first members of the large "baby boom" generation (those born from approximately 1945 to 1965) will begin turning age 65. And a large population with similar interests, concerns, and needs means (among other things) a large consumer group with similar needs and wants. These include specialized medical care, help for daily living activities, and specialized support for dealing with and planning for emotional and end-of-life issues. The resources people turn to for such services are in the hands of professionals such as senior care pharmacists, geriatric social workers, and geriatric nurses.

And that's where you come in. Do you want to provide a service that's in demand by a large number of clients? Do you like the idea of working to make society better? Do the special needs of older people interest you? If your answer to any of these questions is yes, or even maybe, this is the book for you. Although space limitations do not allow us to cover every geriatric care occupation in this book, the careers covered here will give you an idea of the variety of opportunities available in this field.

Each article in *Careers in Focus: Geriatric Care* discusses a particular occupation in detail. The articles appear in Ferguson's *Encyclopedia* of *Careers and Vocational Guidance*. Since the last edition of this book, each article has been updated and revised with the latest information from the U.S. Department of Labor and other sources. Each article is broken down in the following manner.

The **Quick Facts** section provides a brief summary of the career including recommended school subjects, personal skills, work environment, minimum educational requirements, salary ranges, certification or licensing requirements, and employment outlook. This section also provides acronyms and identification numbers for the following government classification indexes: the Dictionary of Occupational Titles (DOT), the Guide for Occupational Exploration (GOE), the National Occupational Classification (NOC) Index, and the Occupational Information Network (O*NET)-Standard Occupational Classification System (SOC) index. The DOT, GOE, and O*NET-SOC indexes have been created by the U.S. government; the NOC index is Canada's career classification system. Readers can use the identification numbers listed in the Quick Facts section to access further information about a career. Print editions of the DOT (*Dictionary of Occupational Titles*. Indianapolis, Ind.: JIST Works, 1991) and GOE (*Guide for Occupational Exploration*. Indianapolis, Ind.: JIST Works, 2001) are available at libraries. Electronic versions of the NOC (http://www23.hrdc-drhc.gc.ca) and O*NET-SOC (http://online.onetcenter.org) are available on the Internet. When no DOT, GOE, NOC, or O*NET-SOC numbers are listed, this means that the U.S. Department of Labor or Human Resources and Skills Development Canada have not created a numerical designation for this career. In this instance, you will see the acronym "N/A," or not available.

The **Overview** section is a brief introductory description of the duties and responsibilities involved in this career. Oftentimes, a career may have a variety of job titles. When this is the case, alternative career titles are presented. Employment statistics are also provided, when available. The **History** section describes the history of the particular job as it relates to the overall development of its industry or field. **The Job** describes the primary and secondary duties of the job. **Requirements** discusses high school and postsecondary education and training requirements, any certification or licensing that is necessary, and other personal requirements for success in the job. **Exploring** offers suggestions on how to gain experience in or knowledge of the particular job before making a firm educational and financial commitment. The focus is on what can be done while still in high school (or in the early years of college) to gain a better understanding of the job. The **Employers** section gives an overview of typical places of employment for the job. **Starting Out** discusses the best ways to land that first job, be it through the college career services office, newspaper ads, Internet employment sites, or personal contact. The **Advancement** section describes what kind of career path to expect from the job and how to get there. **Earnings** lists salary ranges and describes the typical fringe benefits. The **Work Environment** section describes the typical surroundings and conditions of employment—whether indoors or outdoors, noisy or quiet, social or independent. Also discussed are typical hours worked, any seasonal fluctuations, and the stresses and strains of the job. The **Outlook** section summarizes the job in terms of the general economy and industry projections. For the most part, Outlook information is obtained from the U.S. Bureau of Labor Statistics and is supplemented by information gathered from professional associations. Job growth terms follow those used in the *Occupational Outlook Handbook*. Growth described as "much faster than the average" means an increase of 21 percent or more. Growth described as "faster than the average" means an increase of 14 to 20 percent. Growth described as "about as fast as the average" means an increase of 7 to 13 percent. Growth described as "more slowly than the average" means an increase of 3 to 6 percent. "Little or no change" means a decrease of 2 percent to an increase of 2 percent. "Decline" means a decrease of 3 percent or more. Each article ends with **For More Information,** which lists organizations that provide information on training, education, internships, scholarships, and job placement.

Throughout the book you will also find illustrative photographs of some careers, informative sidebars, and interviews with professionals working in the geriatric care field.

As you explore the wide variety of geriatric care careers that are presented in this book, consider which of them might best suit your personality, strengths, and general career goals. Be sure to contact the organizations listed at the end of each article for more information. Good luck with your career exploration!

Adult Day Care Coordinators

QUICK FACTS

School Subjects
Family and consumer science
Psychology
Sociology

Personal Skills
Helping/teaching
Leadership/management

Work Environment
Primarily indoors
Primarily one location

Minimum Education Level
Associate's degree

Salary Range
$18,000 to $55,000 to
$94,000

Certification or Licensing
Required for certain positions

Outlook
Much faster than the average

DOT
354

GOE
N/A

NOC
N/A

O*NET-SOC
N/A

OVERVIEW

Adult day care coordinators, also called *adult day services coordinators,* direct day service programs for adults who have physical or mental impairments or both. Clients of these programs are usually the elderly, although younger people with impairments, such as those recovering from strokes, may also participate in these programs. Coordinators oversee staff members who provide care, meals, and social activities to day care clients, and they serve as liaisons between their centers and their clients' families.

HISTORY

Adult day care had its beginnings in the 1940s in psychiatric hospitals. It started as an effort to help patients who had been released from mental institutions. Over the next 20 years the focus gradually shifted from psychiatric care to other kinds of health maintenance. The landmark publication *Developing Day Care for Older People,* published by the National Council on the Aging (NCOA) in 1972, provided technical assistance for establishing adult day care; by 1978 there were nearly 300 adult day care centers throughout the United States.

In the 1980s, the first Congressional hearing was held on adult day care programs and the Economic Recovery Act was passed, allowing a tax credit to families with elderly members in day care. NCOA established voluntary standards.

According to the National Adult Day Services Association, more than 4,600 adult day centers are currently operating in the United

Did You Know?

- The number of adult day care programs increased by 35 percent from 2002 to 2008.
- Adult day care centers serve more than 150,000 care recipients daily.
- The average adult day care staff-to-recipient ratio is 6:1.

Source: National Adult Day Services Association; National Study of Adult Day Services; The Metlife Market Survey of Adult Day Services & Home Care Costs

States. Nearly 78 percent operate on a nonprofit or public basis, and many are affiliated with larger organizations such as home care, skilled nursing facilities, medical centers, or multipurpose senior organizations.

THE JOB

Adult day care coordinators direct adult day care centers. Although specific duties vary depending on the size of the center and the services it offers, the general responsibility of coordinators is to ensure that their centers provide the necessary care for clients. Such care may include attention to personal hygiene and providing meals, medications, therapies, and social activities.

Although coordinators working in small day care centers may actually perform some services for clients, this is not the norm. Instead, coordinators usually oversee various staff members who provide the caregiving. A large center, for example, might have a nurse, physical therapist, social worker, cook, and several aides. Coordinators are responsible for staff hiring, training, and scheduling. They may meet with staff members either one-on-one or in group sessions to review and discuss plans for the clients.

Overseeing meal planning and preparation is also the responsibility of the adult day services coordinator. In most centers, clients are given a midday meal and usually juices and snacks in the morning and afternoon. Coordinators work with a cook or dietitian to develop well-rounded menus that take into account the nutritional needs of the clients, including any particular restrictions such as diabetic or low-sodium diets. The coordinator may also oversee purchasing and taking inventory of the center's food supply.

The coordinator schedules daily and weekly activities for the day care clients. Depending on the particular needs and abilities of the clients, a recreational schedule might include crafts, games, exercises, reading time, or movies. In some centers, clients are taken on outings to shopping centers, parks, or restaurants. The coordinator plans such outings, arranging for transportation and any reservations or special accommodations that may be necessary. Finally, the coordinator also organizes parties for special events, such as holidays and birthdays.

Finding new activities and visitors for the center is also part of the job. Coordinators might recruit volunteers to teach crafts or music to the clients. Often, religious or civic groups come to such facilities to visit with clients. Some such groups institute buddy programs, in which each group member pairs with a day care client to develop an ongoing relationship. The day care coordinator must authorize and monitor any group visits, activities, or programs.

In addition to planning and overseeing the activities of the center and its clients, the adult day care coordinator also works closely with client family members to make sure that each individual is receiving care that best fits his or her needs. This relationship with the client's family usually begins before the client is placed in the day care center.

When a family is considering placing an elderly relative in day care, they often have many questions about the center and its activities. The coordinator meets with family members to show them the center and explain to them how it is run. The coordinator also gathers information about the potential client, including names and phone numbers of doctors and people to contact in case of emergency, lists of medications taken with instructions on when and how they should be administered, and information on allergies, food choices, and daily habits and routines.

After the client is placed in the center, the coordinator may meet periodically with the client's family to update them on how the client is responding to the day care setting. If necessary, the coordinator may advise the family about social services, such as home health care, and refer them to other providers.

Adult day care coordinators may have other duties, depending on the center and how it is owned and operated. For example, they may be responsible for developing and adhering to a budget for the center. In centers licensed or certified by the state, coordinators may ensure that their centers remain in compliance with the regulations and necessary documentation. They may also be responsible for general bookkeeping, bill payment, and office management.

In addition to supervising centers, coordinators may also promote and advertise to the community. They may help with fund-raising, prepare press releases, and speak to various service clubs.

REQUIREMENTS

High School

While you are in high school, you should take classes that prepare you for postsecondary training. These include mathematics, business, family and consumer science classes as well as science classes, such as biology. To improve your understanding of people, take history, psychology, and sociology classes. Because communication is an important skill, English and speech classes are also good choices.

Postsecondary Training

Because this is a relatively new and growing field, there are no national standards to follow for becoming an adult day care coordinator. Some people have learned their skills on the job; others have taken courses in home nursing or health care; still others have completed associate's or bachelor's degrees in areas such as health and human services. As the need for and popularity of day care services continue to grow, more employers will begin to expect coordinators to have at least some formal education.

Many employers prefer to hire candidates who meet the standards set by the National Adult Day Services Association. In order to meet these standards, a coordinator must have a bachelor's degree in health or social services or a related field, with one year's supervisory experience in a social or health services setting. In preparation for such a career, a college student might choose occupational, recreational, or rehabilitation therapy, or social work or human development. An increasingly popular major for potential adult day care coordinators is gerontology, or geriatrics.

The Association for Gerontology in Higher Education publishes the *Directory of Educational Programs in Gerontology and Geriatrics,* which contains information on programs available from the associate's to the postdoctorate level. Although specific courses vary from school to school, most programs consist of classes in social gerontology, biology and physiology of aging, psychology of aging, and sociology of aging. In addition to these four core classes, most programs offer elective courses in such areas as social policy, community services, nutrition and exercise, diversity in aging, health issues, death and dying, and ethics and life extension.

A practicum or field placement is also a part of most gerontology programs. This allows students to obtain experience working with both well-functioning elderly people and those with age-related disabilities.

Certification or Licensing

The National Certification Council for Activity Professionals offers certification to activity directors. See the end of the article for contact information.

Regulations can vary by state. In some states, for example, the agency that a coordinator works for must be licensed or certified by the state health department. Any adult day care center that receives payment from Medicare or from other government programs must be certified by the state department of health. In these cases, licensing requirements may include requirements for coordinators and other staff members. The trend is toward stricter standards.

Other Requirements

Regardless of what level of education a prospective coordinator has, there are certain personal characteristics that are necessary for success in this field. Compassion and an affinity for the elderly and disabled are vital, as are patience and the desire to help others. You should also be organized and able to manage other workers effectively. Communication skills are very important since you will be working with staff, clients, regulatory agencies, and clients' families.

EXPLORING

There are several ways you can learn more about the career of adult day care coordinator. The first and easiest way is to check your local library for books or articles on aging in order to learn more about the elderly, their issues, and the services available to them. Resources are also available on the Internet. Next, visit a nursing home or adult day care center in order to experience firsthand what it is like to spend time with and interact with elderly people. Arrange to talk with staff members and the center's coordinator to find out what their day-to-day jobs are like. Your high school counselor may also be able to arrange for a coordinator to give a career talk at your school. Finally, get a volunteer position or part-time job in such a facility. This would allow you to gauge your aptitude for a career in adult day care work.

EMPLOYERS

Adult day care coordinators work at adult day care centers. These may be small or large. It is estimated that there are more than 4,600 adult day care centers currently operating in the United States. Most of them are operated on a nonprofit or public basis, and many are affiliated with large organizations such as nursing homes, hospitals, or multipurpose senior organizations. Standards and work environments vary.

STARTING OUT

In looking for a position as an adult day care coordinator, candidates should first locate and contact all such programs in the area. Checking the local Yellow Pages under Nursing Homes, Residential Care Facilities, Aging Services, or Senior Citizens Services should provide a list of leads. The job seeker might either send a resume and cover letter or call these potential employers directly. Prospective coordinators should also watch for job openings listed in area newspapers and on organizations' Web sites.

Another means of finding job leads is to become affiliated with a professional association, such as the American Geriatrics Society, the American Association of Homes and Services for the Aging, the Gerontological Society of America, or the National Council on Aging. Many such organizations have monthly or quarterly newsletters that list job opportunities. Some may even have job banks or referral services.

Job seekers who have received associate's or bachelor's degrees should also check with the career services offices at their colleges or universities.

ADVANCEMENT

Because the field of aging-related services continues to grow, the potential for advancement for adult day care coordinators is good. Some coordinators advance by transferring to a larger center that pays better wages. Others eventually start their own centers. Still others advance by moving into management positions in other, similar social service organizations, such as nursing homes, hospices, or government agencies on aging.

An adult day care coordinator might choose to return to school and complete a higher degree, often a master's degree in social work. For those who choose this option, there are many career opportunities in the field of social services. Social workers, for example, work with individuals and families dealing with AIDS, cancer, or other debilitating illnesses. They also work for agencies offering various types of counseling, rehabilitation, or crisis intervention.

EARNINGS

Starting salaries for this position depend partly on the experience and education of the coordinator and partly upon the size and location of the day care center. Larger centers located in metropolitan areas tend to offer the highest wages.

According to the Association for Gerontology in Higher Education, beginning annual salaries range from $18,000 to $31,000 for persons with a bachelor's degree and little experience. Generally, coordinators who do not have a bachelor's degree can expect to earn somewhat less. Experienced coordinators with a bachelor's degree employed in large, well-funded centers may earn from $32,000 to $94,000 annually, with an estimated median salary of $55,000.

In addition to salary, some coordinators are also offered a benefits package, which typically includes health insurance, paid vacation and sick days, and a retirement plan.

WORK ENVIRONMENT

Most adult day care centers have a schedule that corresponds to standard business hours. Most coordinators work a 40-hour week, Monday through Friday, with weekends off.

The coordinator's work environment will vary depending on the size and type of center he or she supervises. Some centers are fairly institutional, resembling children's day care centers or nursing homes. Others have a more residential feel, being carpeted and furnished like a private home. Regardless of the furnishings, the center is typically clean, well lit, and equipped with ramps, rails, and other devices that ensure the safety of clients.

Part of the coordinator's day may be spent in the center's common areas with clients and staff. He or she may also spend time working in an on-site office. If the staff members take clients on outings, the coordinator may accompany them.

Coordinators are on their feet much of the time, ensuring that meals and activities run smoothly and helping staff members when necessary. Attire for the job varies from center to center, ranging from very casual to standard office wear. Most coordinators, however, wear clothing that is comfortable and allows them freedom of movement.

Regardless of the size of the center, coordinators spend the majority of their time working with people, both staff members and day care clients. Working with clients is often very trying. Many of them may have had a stroke or have Alzheimer's disease, and they may be confused, uncooperative, or even hostile. The job may also be emotionally taxing for the coordinator who becomes attached to his or her clients. Most adults who use a day care center are elderly or permanently disabled; for this reason, day care staff must frequently deal with the decline and eventual death of their clients.

OUTLOOK

The outlook for all human services workers, and adult day care coordinators in particular, is expected to be excellent through 2018, growing at a rate that is much faster than the average. The main reason for this is that the senior citizen population is growing rapidly. According to a study conducted by the U.S. Census Bureau, by 2050 there will be 82 million older persons in the United States, which is more than twice the number that existed in 1999. Coupled with this growing elderly population will be a decreasing number of caregivers because of increased divorce rates, smaller families, delayed child-bearing trends, and more men and women in the workforce. Given these projections, adult day care will be used more frequently as a cost-efficient and preferable alternative to nursing homes.

FOR MORE INFORMATION

For information on careers and aging and services for the elderly, contact
American Association of Homes and Services for the Aging
2519 Connecticut Avenue, NW
Washington, DC 20008-1520
Tel: 202-783-2242
E-mail: info@aahsa.org
http://www.aahsa.org

AGHE, a section of the Gerontological Society of America, promotes education in the field of aging and offers a directory of gerontology and geriatrics programs.
Association for Gerontology in Higher Education (AGHE)
1220 L Street, NW, Suite 901
Washington, DC 20005
Tel: 202-289-9806
http://www.aghe.org

For career information and student resources, contact
Gerontological Society of America
1220 L Street NW, Suite 901
Washington, DC 20005
Tel: 202-842-1275
http://www.geron.org

For information on the history of adult day service and day service facts, contact
National Adult Day Services Association
85 South Washington, Suite 316
Seattle WA 98104-3405
Tel: 877-745-1440
E-mail: info@nadsa.org
http://www.nadsa.org

This organization can provide information on services, including adult day care, available across the country.
National Association of Area Agencies on Aging
1730 Rhode Island Avenue, NW, Suite 1200
Washington, DC 20036-3109
Tel: 202-872-0888
http://www.n4a.org

For information on certification, contact
National Certification Council for Activity Professionals
PO Box 62589
Virginia Beach, VA 23466-2589
Tel: 757-552-0653
http://www.nccap.org

To learn about developments and current issues in the aging field, visit the following Web site:
National Council on Aging
1901 L Street, NW, 4th Floor
Washington, DC 20036-3540
Tel: 202-479-1200
http://www.ncoa.org

For comprehensive information about geriatric care careers, visit
Careers in Aging: Resources for Developing Your Career in Aging
http://www.aghe.org/templates/System/details asp?id=40634 &PID=500215

INTERVIEW

Beth Meyer-Arnold is the director of adult day services at Luther Manor, an accredited continuing care retirement community in Wauwatosa, Wisconsin, that serves more than 800 residents. She is also a board member of the National Adult Day Services Association and the Alzheimer's Association of Southeastern Wisconsin. Beth discussed her career with the editors of Careers in Focus: Geriatric Care.

Q. What made you want to enter this career?

A. My mother is an R.N. and she was my role model. Since I was about seven years old, I was dreaming about helping people stay healthy. I graduated from Marquette University College of Nursing and worked in an acute care hospital for 10 years, in many roles, from staff nurse to supervisor of the emergency room and intensive care unit. I always gravitated to the older patients. They were more complicated and needed more thought and teamwork. However, I became more and more frustrated with the acute care hospital system in which older adults were basically treated as if they were "senile," incontinent, hard of hearing, and unable to make decisions for themselves. I tried to work through committees, to highlight the importance of having a geriatric expert on staff, to help nurses to understand the complexities of the older patient, as well as the gifts they could bring. The hospital was not able to give any time or resources to focus on the older patient. They were too busy with the neonatal nursery and the cardiac care system. I decided then and there to go back to graduate school in gerontology and community health nursing. I decided that I would need to develop programs and services for older adults from the long-term care system. I have been doing that now for more than 20 years!

Q. Can you please describe a day in your life on the job?

A. I am an administrator of home- and community-based services for a senior living community that has residential services, independent living, assisted living, and nursing home care as well. The community services include adult day services, parish nursing, senior centers, case management, and respite services and early memory loss classes. I am the administrator of the adult day, respite, and early memory loss services.

I am responsible for the administration of this program, so I am the person who hires, trains, and provides guidance to the staff. I coordinate partnerships and students and trainees and volunteers, and develop new services. I am responsible for new program development, including fund development, if needed. I am also responsible for contributing to the administration team of senior living community, speaking for the needs and wants of those of our constituents who are living in the community.

I am also responsible for participating on community commissions, committees, boards, and advisory councils that advance the quality of services for the older adults that we serve.

I am a preceptor for four universities and coordinate experiences for undergraduate and graduate students. I am also responsible for the budget, so I have financial oversight for my programs.

We start our day in a report with all the staff. I then attend meetings, [participate in] phone conferences, meet with management staff, and greet employees, participants, and volunteers. I assist the staff nurses with problem solving for our participants, using my geriatric nursing advanced practice as much as I can!

Q. What are some of the pros and cons of your job?
A. Managing employees can be very rewarding, but also very stressful! Working with older adults can also be challenging due to the incredible vulnerabilities they face and the tenacity to continue to live in their homes and care for themselves. It is rewarding when they can be successful and you were a part of it.

Q. What are the most important personal and professional qualities for people in your career?
A. Creativity and teamwork—hands down! Learning how to open your mind to be able to live in theirs'—both older adults and other employees.

Q. What activities would you suggest to high school students who are interested in this career?
A. Check out your high school or church youth group to see if they have a services learning partnership with a local adult day center or senior living community. Volunteer! And do it on a regular basis, so you get to know the older adults who attend. You will start to have relationships with them, and then you will be hooked!

Q. What advice would you give to young people who are interested in the field?
A. Ask lots of questions while you are volunteering. Find out the wide variety of careers that are available in senior services. Find out where your passion is—is it in the social services, health services, or administration? It may be marketing, or medical services or chaplain services. It could be maintenance, food service, or transportation.

Talk to older adults. Find a mentor. You will walk away with more gifts than you gave them!

Creative Arts Therapists

OVERVIEW

Creative arts therapists treat and rehabilitate people with mental, physical, and emotional disabilities. They use the creative processes of music, art, dance/movement, drama, psychodrama, and poetry in their therapy sessions to determine the underlying causes of problems and to help patients achieve therapeutic goals. Creative arts therapists usually specialize in one particular type of therapeutic activity. The specific objectives of the therapeutic activities vary according to the needs of the patient and the setting of the therapy program.

HISTORY

Creative arts therapy programs are fairly recent additions to the health care field. Although many theories of mental and physical therapy have existed for centuries, it has been only in the last 75 years or so that health care professionals have truly realized the healing powers of music, art, dance, and other forms of artistic self-expression.

Art therapy is based on the idea that people who cannot discuss their problems with words must have another outlet for self-expression. In the early 1900s, psychiatrists began to look more closely at their patients' artwork, realizing that there could be links between the emotional or psychological illness and the art. Sigmund Freud even did some preliminary research into the artistic expression of his patients.

A music therapist performs for residents of an assisted living facility.
(*Dave Martin, AP Photo*)

In the 1930s, art educators discovered that children often expressed their thoughts better with pictures and role-playing than they did through verbalization. Children often do not know the words they need to explain how they feel or how to make their needs known to adults. Researchers began to look into art as a way to treat children who were traumatized by abuse, neglect, illness, or other physical or emotional disabilities.

During and after World War II, the Department of Veterans Affairs (VA) developed and organized various art, music, and dance activities for patients in VA hospitals. These activities had a dramatic effect on the physical and mental well-being of World War II veterans, and creative arts therapists began to help treat and rehabilitate patients in other health care settings.

Because of early breakthroughs with children and veterans, the number of arts therapists has increased greatly over the past few decades, and the field has expanded to include drama, psychodrama, and poetry, in addition to the original areas of music, art, and dance. Today, creative arts therapists work with diverse populations of patients in a wide range of facilities (from small children to senior citizens), and they focus on the specific needs of a vast spectrum of disorders and disabilities. Colleges and universities offer degree programs in many types of therapies, and national associations for registering and certifying creative arts therapists work to monitor training programs and to ensure the professional integrity of the therapists working in the various fields.

THE JOB

Tapping a power related to dreaming, creative arts therapy taps into the subconscious and gives people a mode of expression in an uncensored environment. This is important because before patients can begin to heal, they must first identify their feelings. Once they recognize their feelings, they can begin to develop an understanding of the relationship between their feelings and their behavior.

The main goal of a creative arts therapist is to improve the client's physical, mental, and emotional health. Before therapists who work with the elderly begin any treatment, they meet with a team of other health care professionals, such as geriatric nurses, geriatricians, physical therapists, and geriatric social workers. After determining the strength, limitations, and interests of their client, they create a program to promote positive change and growth. The creative arts therapist continues to confer with the other health care workers as the program progresses, and alters the program according to the client's progress. How these goals are reached depends on the unique specialty of the therapist in question.

Creative arts therapists work with all age groups: young children, adolescents, adults, and senior citizens. They can work in individual, group, or family sessions. The approach of the therapist, however, depends on the specific needs of the client or group. For example, a music therapist working with a stroke victim would first assess his or her current level of functioning and physical and mental health before and after the stroke and establish short- and long-term goals to regain and improve functioning. Therapists who work with the elderly must accept the fact that a patient may never completely recover or only show marginal improvement.

To reach their patients, creative arts therapists can use a variety of mediums, including visual art, music, dance, drama, or poetry or other kinds of creative writing. Creative arts therapists use many tools in their sessions, including clay, chalk, paint, musical instruments, or paper. Therapists themselves, are perhaps the most important tool. They have to use their eyes and ears to pay constant attention to the behavior of patients before, during, and after the session. That behavior is as important as the art work that they create.

Creative arts therapists usually specialize in a specific practice area, becoming a music therapist, art therapist, dance therapist, drama therapist, or poetry therapist.

Music therapists use musical lessons and activities to improve a patient's self-confidence and self-awareness, to relieve states of depression (in elderly people with a chronic illness or those who are dying), and to improve physical dexterity or mental acuity. For example, a music therapist treating a patient with Alzheimer's might play songs from the patient's past in order to stimulate long- and short-term memory, soothe feelings of agitation, and increase a sense of reality. A music therapist may work with a hospice patient to identify his or her musical tastes and then play the music on a musical instrument or through an MP3 player or portable music system.

Art therapists use art in much the same manner. The art therapist may encourage and teach patients to express their thoughts, feelings, and anxieties via sketching, drawing, painting, or sculpting. Patients may be encouraged to use art to illustrate their frustration with being ill or fear of dying.

Dance/movement therapists develop and conduct dance/movement sessions to help improve the physical, mental, and emotional health of their patients. Dance and movement therapy is also used as a way of assessing a patient's progress toward reaching therapeutic goals.

Drama therapists use role-playing, pantomime (the telling of a story by the use of expressive body or facial movements), puppetry, improvisation, and original scripted dramatization to evaluate and treat patients.

Poetry therapists and *bibliotherapists* use the written and spoken word to treat patients.

REQUIREMENTS

High School
To become a creative arts therapist, you will need a bachelor's degree, so take a college preparatory curriculum while in high school. You should become as proficient as possible with the methods and tools related to the type of creative arts therapy you wish to pursue. When therapists work with patients they must be able to concentrate completely on the patient rather than on learning how to use tools or techniques. For example, if you want to become involved in music therapy, you need to be familiar with musical instruments as well as theory. A good starting point for a music therapist is to study piano or guitar.

In addition to courses such as drama, art, music, and English, you should consider taking an introductory class in psychology. Also, a communication class will give you an understanding of the various ways people communicate, both verbally and nonverbally.

Postsecondary Training

To become a creative arts therapist you must earn at least a bachelor's degree, usually in the area in which you wish to specialize. For example, those studying to be art therapists typically have undergraduate degrees in studio art, art education, or psychology with a strong emphasis on art courses as well.

In most cases, however, you will also need a graduate degree before you can gain certification as a professional or advance in your chosen field. Requirements for admission to graduate schools vary by program, so you would be wise to contact the graduate programs you are interested in to find out about their admissions policies. For some fields you may be required to submit a portfolio of your work along with the written application. Professional organizations can be a good source of information regarding high-quality programs. For example, both the American Art Therapy Association and the American Music Therapy Association provide lists of schools that meet their standards for approval. (Contact information for both associations is listed at the end of this article.)

In graduate school, your study of psychology and the arts field you are interested in will be in-depth. Classes for someone seeking a master's in art therapy, for example, may include group psychotherapy, foundation of creativity theory, assessment and treatment planning, and art therapy presentation. In addition to classroom study you will also complete an internship or supervised practicum (that is, work with clients). Depending on your program, you may also need to write a thesis or present a final artistic project before receiving your degree.

Certification or Licensing

Typically, the nationally recognized association or certification board specific to your field of choice offers registration and certification. For example, the Art Therapy Credentials Board (ATCB) offers registration and certification to art therapists, and the American Dance Therapy Association offers certification to dance therapists. In general, requirements for registration include completing an approved therapy program and having a certain amount of experience working with clients. Requirements for higher levels of registration or certification generally involve having additional work experience and passing a written exam.

For a specific example, consider the certification process for an art therapist: An art therapist may receive the designation art therapist registered from the ATCB after completing a graduate program and having some experience working with clients. The next level, then, is to become a board-certified art therapist by passing a written exam.

To retain certification status, therapists must complete a certain amount of continuing education.

Many registered creative arts therapists also hold additional licenses in other fields, such as social work, education, mental health, or marriage and family therapy. In some states, creative arts therapists need licensing depending on their place of work. For specific information on licensing in your field, you will need to check with your state's licensing board. Creative arts therapists are also often members of other professional associations, including the American Psychological Association, the American Association for Marriage and Family Therapy, and the American Counseling Association.

Other Requirements

To succeed in this line of work, you should have a strong desire to help others seek positive change in their lives. All types of creative arts therapists must be able to work well with other people—both patients and other health professionals—in the development and implementation of therapy programs. You must have the patience and the stamina to teach and practice therapy with patients for whom progress is often very slow because of their various physical and emotional disorders. A therapist must always keep in mind that even a tiny amount of progress might be extremely significant for some patients and their families. A good sense of humor is also a valuable trait.

EXPLORING

There are many ways to explore the possibility of a career as a creative arts therapist. Contact professional associations for information on therapy careers. Talk with people working in the creative arts therapy field and perhaps arrange to observe a creative arts therapy session. Look for part-time or summer jobs or volunteer at a hospital, clinic, nursing home, or any of a number of health care facilities. These opportunities may help provide insight into the nature of creative arts therapy, including both its rewards and demands. Such experience can be very valuable in deciding if you are suited to the inherent frustrations of a therapy career.

EMPLOYERS

Creative arts therapists usually work as members of an interdisciplinary health care team that may include physicians, nurses, social workers, psychiatrists, and psychologists. Although often employed in hospitals, therapists also work in rehabilitation centers, nursing homes, day treatment facilities, shelters for battered women, pain and stress management clinics, substance abuse programs, hospices, and correctional facilities. Others maintain their own private practices. Many creative arts therapists work with children in grammar and high schools, either as therapists or art teachers. Some arts therapists teach or conduct research in the creative arts at colleges and universities.

STARTING OUT

After earning a bachelor's degree in a particular field, you should complete your certification, which may include an internship or assistantship. Unpaid training internships often can lead to a first job in the field. Graduates can use the career services office at their college or university to help them find positions in the creative arts therapy field. Many professional associations also compile lists of job openings to assist their members.

Creative arts therapists who are new to the field might consider doing volunteer work at a nonprofit community organization, correctional facility, or neighborhood association to gain some practical experience. Therapists who want to start their own practice can host group therapy sessions in their homes. Creative arts therapists may also wish to associate with other members of the complementary/alternative health care field in order to gain experience and build a client base.

ADVANCEMENT

With more experience, therapists can move into supervisory, administrative, and teaching positions. Often, the supervision of interns can resemble a therapy session. The interns will discuss their feelings and ask questions they may have regarding their work with clients. How did they handle their clients? What were the reactions to what their clients said or did? What could they be doing to help more? The supervising therapist helps the interns become competent creative arts therapists.

Many therapists have represented the profession internationally at association or educational conferences. Others write articles and books about creative arts therapy or appear as experts on television and radio. Raising the public and professional awareness of creative arts therapy is an important concern for many therapists.

EARNINGS

A therapist's annual salary depends on experience, level of training, education, and specialty. Working on a hospital staff or being self-employed also affects annual income. According to the American Art Therapy Association (AATA), entry-level art therapists earn annual salaries of approximately $32,000. Median annual salaries are about $38,000 to $48,000, and AATA reports that top earnings for salaried administrators ranged from $50,000 and $80,000 annually. Those who have Ph.D.'s and are licensed for private practice can earn between $85 and $120 per hour, according to AATA. However, those in private practice must pay professional expenses such as insurance and office rental.

Salaries for music therapists vary based on experience, level of training, and education. Music therapists earned average annual salaries of $46,417 in 2008, according to the American Music Therapy Association. The average annual salary for music therapists in geriatric facilities was $46,971.

Benefits depend on the employer but generally include paid vacation time, health insurance, and paid sick days. Those who are in private practice must provide their own benefits.

WORK ENVIRONMENT

Most creative arts therapists work a typical 40-hour, five-day workweek; at times, however, they may have to work extra hours. The number of patients under a therapist's care depends on the specific employment setting. Although many therapists work in hospitals, they may also be employed in such facilities as clinics, rehabilitation centers, children's homes, schools, and nursing homes. Some therapists maintain service contracts with several facilities. For instance, a therapist might work two days a week at a hospital, one day at a nursing home, and the rest of the week at a rehabilitation center.

Most buildings are pleasant, comfortable, and clean places in which to work. Experienced creative arts therapists might choose to be self-employed, working with patients in their own studios. In such a case, the therapist might work more irregular hours to accommodate patient schedules. Other therapists might maintain a combination of service contract work with one or more facilities in addition to a private caseload of clients referred to them by other health care professionals. Whether therapists work on service contracts with various facilities or maintain private practices, they must deal with all of the business and administrative details and worries that go along with being self-employed.

OUTLOOK

The American Art Therapy Association notes that art therapy is a growing field. Demand for new therapists is created as medical professionals and the general public become aware of the benefits gained through art therapies. Although enrollment in college therapy programs is increasing, new graduates are usually able to find jobs. In cases where an individual is unable to find a full-time position, a therapist might obtain service contracts for part-time work at several facilities.

The American Music Therapy Association predicts a promising future for the field of music therapy. Demand for music therapists will grow as medical professionals and the general public become aware of the benefits gained through music therapy.

Job openings in facilities such as nursing homes should continue to increase as the elderly population grows over the next few decades. Advances in medical technology and the recent practice of early discharge from hospitals should also create new opportunities in managed care facilities, chronic pain clinics, and cancer care facilities. The demand for therapists of all types should continue to increase as more people become aware of the need to help disabled patients in creative ways.

FOR MORE INFORMATION

For more detailed information about your field of interest, contact the following organizations:

American Art Therapy Association
225 North Fairfax Street
Alexandria, VA 22314-2646
Tel: 888-290-0878
E-mail: info@arttherapy.org
http://www.arttherapy.org

American Dance Therapy Association
10632 Little Patuxent Parkway, Suite 108
Columbia, MD 21044-3263
Tel: 410-997-4040
E-mail: info@adta.org
http://www.adta.org

American Music Therapy Association
8455 Colesville Road, Suite 1000
Silver Spring, MD 20910-3392
Tel: 301-589-3300
E-mail: info@musictherapy.org
http://www.musictherapy.org

American Society of Group Psychotherapy and Psychodrama
301 North Harrison Street, Suite 508
Princeton, NJ 08540-3512
Tel: 609-737-8500
E-mail: asgpp@asgpp.org
http://www.asgpp.org

National Association for Drama Therapy
44365 Premier Plaza, Suite 220
Ashburn, VA 20147-5058
Tel: 888-416-7167
E-mail: nadt.office@nadt.org
http://www.nadt.org

National Association for Poetry Therapy
c/o Center for Education, Training & Holistic Approaches
777 East Atlantic Avenue, #243
Delray Beach, FL 33483-5360
Tel: 866-844-6278
http://www.poetrytherapy.org

For an overview of the various types of art therapy, visit the coalition's Web site.
National Coalition of Creative Arts Therapies Associations
c/o American Music Therapy Association
8455 Colesville Road, Suite 1000
Silver Spring, MD 20910-3392
Tel: 201-224-9146
http://www.nccata.org

Elder Law Attorneys

OVERVIEW

Lawyers, or *attorneys,* work in our legal system as advocates and advisers. As advocates, they represent the rights of their clients in trials and depositions or in front of administrative and government bodies. As advisers, attorneys counsel clients on how the law affects business or personal decisions, such as the purchase of property or the creation of a will. Lawyers can represent individuals, businesses, and corporations. *Elder law attorneys* are lawyers who specialize in providing legal services for the elderly and, in some cases, the disabled. Unlike other lawyers who deal with one field of law, such as tax lawyers, elder law attorneys often deal with several fields of law when providing services to their clients. Some of the most common elder law issues include guardianship or conservatorship, public benefits (Medicaid, Medicare, and Social Security), probate and estate planning, health and long-term care planning, and elder abuse cases. The National Academy of Elder Law Attorneys (NAELA) reports that its current membership is 4,400. In addition, there are thousands of attorneys who practice elder law as a part of a law practice that encompasses a range of other areas.

HISTORY

Over the centuries, societies have built up systems of law that have been studied and drawn upon by later governments. The earliest known law is the Code of Hammurabi, developed about 1800 B.C. by the ruler of the Sumerians. Another early set of laws was the Law of Moses, also known as the Ten Commandments. Every set

What an Elder Law Attorney Needs to Know

The Board of Certification of the National Elder Law Foundation requires that certified elder law attorneys be knowledgeable in the following subjects:

- Health and long-term care planning
- Public benefits (Medicare, Medicaid, Social Security)
- Surrogate decision making (including powers of attorney and guardianship)
- Legal capacity of older persons
- Estate issues, including wills, trusts, and probate of an estate

The board also expects certified elder law attorneys to be capable of recognizing and handling the issues often involved in counseling and representing older people, such as abuse or neglect, insurance, housing, long-term care, and retirement issues. Elder law attorneys must also be aware of public and private nonlegal resources that are available for older persons, and they must know when and how to recommend such services.

For more information, visit http://www.nelf.org.

of laws, no matter when it was introduced, has been accompanied by the need for someone to explain those laws and help others live under them.

Much modern European law was organized and refined by legal experts assembled by Napoleon; their body of law was known as the Napoleonic Code. English colonists coming to America brought English common law, which influenced the development of much of American law. As the population in the country grew and the number of businesses increased, those who knew the law were in high demand. The two main kinds of law are civil and criminal, but many other specialty areas are also prevalent today. When our country was young, most lawyers were general law practitioners; they knew and worked with all the laws for their clients. Today, as laws have grown more complex, an increasing number of lawyers specialize and limit their practices to certain areas, such as tax law, corporate law, and intellectual property law.

In the 20th century, the number of Americans over the age of 65 increased dramatically. One significant reason for this increase was medical and technological advances that extended life spans. As the older population became larger, its members began to experience problems and have concerns that affected all of society, including financing the postretirement years, the increased need for nursing homes and medical/geriatric care, the legal and ethical issues regarding the care of individuals with diminished capabilities, and the frequent difficulty of getting the appropriate public benefits. Senior citizens who may never have seen an attorney in their lives can find themselves in need of legal advice and advocacy. Out of necessity, elder law has developed to meet their needs. In addition, one of the largest generations in our country's history—the "baby boomers" who were born between 1945 and 1965—are becoming a part of this older generation (in the next few years through the 2030s). As this large generation ages, the demand for elder law attorneys should increase.

THE JOB

Lawyers can give legal advice and, when necessary, represent their clients' interests in court. Regardless of their area of expertise, an attorney's job is to help clients know and understand their legal rights and to help them assert those rights before a judge, jury, government agency, or other legal forum, such as an arbitration panel.

Elder law attorneys focus on the needs of their elderly clients, using a variety of legal tools and techniques to meet their goals in an efficient, fiscally responsible, and legally sound manner. Elder law attorneys deal with the whole of the legal needs of their clients. Because of this, their responsibilities are many. They may help one client with estate planning; they may counsel another client about planning for mental incapacity and compose an alternative decision-making document that will allow another family member, for example, to make decisions about that client's health care; and they may assist yet another client in planning for possible long-term care needs, including nursing home care. Locating the appropriate type of care, coordinating private and public resources to finance the cost of care, and working to ensure the client's right to quality care are all part of the elder law practice.

Elder law lawyers must know the law's position on a variety of issues, including health and long-term care planning, surrogate decision making (that is, when the client has appointed someone, most likely a relative, to make financial or other decisions when the client is unable to), obtain public benefits (including Medicaid, Medicare, and Social Security), manage diminished capacity (such as when the client can no longer think clearly), and the conservation and administration of the older person's estate (including wills, trusts, and probate). In advising about these matters, elder law attorneys must know about the tax consequences for clients when they decide on a certain action (such as putting money in a trust); attorneys must also recognize when they need to seek out more sophisticated tax information from an expert and do so for the best interests of their clients. In addition, elder law attorneys must be able to recognize cases of abuse, neglect, and exploitation of an older client. An elder law attorney must also be familiar with professional and nonlegal resources and services that are publicly and privately available to meet the needs of the older person. Elder law lawyers can then refer clients to these resources, which may include adult day care centers, community transportation, and food services. Elder law encompasses more than just legal planning; it deals with a larger realm of life planning.

In many cases, a crisis is what brings a new client to an elder law attorney. Common situations include middle-income families concerned about paying for a parent's long-term care and nursing home care; families with an older member whose ability to think clearly and live independently is diminishing; older people wanting to ensure their wishes are respected when their health deteriorates; families struggling with retirement and/or assisted-living decisions, contracts, and expenses; and families or seniors faced with issues of age discrimination, exploitation, or abuse.

Elder law attorneys must conduct their practices ethically. They must understand their clients, know which confidences can be shared with which family members, and know when and how to seek other professionals, whether about medical, financial, insurance, or tax issues, to best meet the needs of the clients. The attorney must also recognize situations where a client's wishes clash with those of the family and then determine the best way of handling the issues to best serve the client.

REQUIREMENTS

High School

To become a lawyer you will need to get a college degree and a law degree after you graduate from high school. To start preparing for this later education and career, take a college preparatory curriculum, including math, science, and even a foreign language, while in high school. Be sure to take courses in social studies, government, history, and economics to prepare for law studies. English courses are also important for building your writing, researching, and speaking skills. And because lawyers often use technology to research and interpret the law, take advantage of any computer-related classes or experience you can get. Even surfing the Internet can provide experience in doing research online.

Postsecondary Training

To enter any law school approved by the American Bar Association, you must satisfactorily complete at least three, and usually four, years of college work. Most law schools do not specify any particular courses for prelaw education. The traditional majors for college students intending to pursue a postgraduate law degree are history, English, philosophy, political science, economics, and business. Other successful law students have focused their undergraduate studies in areas as diverse as art, music theory, computer science, engineering, nursing, and education. A college student planning to specialize in elder law might also take courses significantly related to that area, such as social sciences, psychology, economics, and courses related to health care.

To gain admission to law school, most programs require applicants to take the Law School Admission Test (LSAT). The LSAT tests students on analytical thinking, writing, and problem-solving skills. Most full-time law degree programs take three years to complete. There are currently 200 ABA-approved law schools in the United States. State authorities approve additional programs, many of them part-time or night school programs that can be completed in four years. Contact law schools you are interested in to find out specific requirements for their programs. College counselors and professors may also be valuable sources of information.

The first year of typical law school programs consists of required courses, such as legal writing and research, contracts, criminal law, constitutional law, torts, and property. First-year law students are required to read and study thousands of legal cases. The second and third years are usually focused on specialized courses of interest to the student. In the case of elder law, students might take course work in public policy, health law, medical ethics, and geriatrics.

Upon completing law school, students usually receive the (J.D.) degree or bachelor of laws (LL.B.) degree.

Certification or Licensing

To obtain a law license, lawyers (regardless of their specialization) must be admitted to the bar association of the state in which they will practice. Bar admission standards in most states require that students graduate from an approved law school and that they pass a bar examination in the state in which they intend to practice. These exams, usually lasting two days, have questions about various areas of the law, such as constitutional law and criminal law. The tests may also include an essay section and a professional responsibility section. It is important to note, however, that each state sets its own standards for taking the bar exam, and a few states allow exceptions to the educational requirements. For example, a small number of states allow a person who has spent several years reading law in a law office and has some law school experience to take the state bar exam. A few states allow people who have completed law study through correspondence programs to take the bar. In addition, some states require that newly graduated lawyers serve a period of clerkship in an established law firm before they are eligible to take the bar examination. Because of such variations, you will need to contact the bar examiners board of your state for specific information on its requirements.

Specialized voluntary certification is available for elder law attorneys. The National Elder Law Foundation (NELF) offers certification to attorneys who have been in practice five years or longer, have spent at least 16 hours per week (over three years) practicing elder law, have handled at least 60 elder law matters, and have had at least 45 hours of continuing legal education in elder law. To obtain certification, applicants must also pass an examination. After five years, certified attorneys must be recertified to maintain their status.

Other Requirements

All lawyers have to be effective communicators, work well with people, and be able to find creative solutions to problems, such as complex court cases. Elder lawyers, however, need to have some special skills and personality characteristics. They need to understand how aging affects the mind and body, how conflicts can arise among family members regarding the best interests of an elderly member, and how the family's wishes sometimes are in conflict with those of the older person. This work requires perceptiveness, ethics, and diplomacy. Elder law attorneys must also be good listeners and seek to understand the goals of their clients. Family members may often have differing opinions and agendas, and it is important to remember who your client is.

EXPLORING

You can explore this profession by finding out more about being a lawyer and by gaining experience working with the elderly. To learn more about the legal profession in general, sit in on some trials at your local or state courthouse. Watch the lawyers and take note of what they do. Write down questions you have and terms or actions you don't understand so you can research them later. Work with your counselor to set up an information interview with a lawyer willing to answer questions about the career. You may also be able to "job shadow" this person for part of a workday or more. By doing this, you can see some of the typical daily work of a lawyer. You may even be able to help with some tasks, such as filing.

The Internet is also a good source of information. You can go to law-related sites to learn more about legal terminology, current court cases, and the field of law in general. Some sites that would be particularly beneficial to visit include those of the American Bar Association, NAELA, and NELF. (See the end of this article for their Web addresses.) You can also try to get part-time or summer work in a lawyer's office. You may only answer phones, file office papers, or type letters, but this work will give you excellent exposure to the profession.

It will also be important for you to get experience working with the elderly, either on a paid or a volunteer basis. Contact local nursing homes, senior centers, and volunteer groups providing services, such as Meals on Wheels, to find out what opportunities are available. By working with the elderly population, you will start to learn about their specific needs, concerns, and opinions.

EMPLOYERS

NAELA reports that its current membership is 4,400. The majority of practicing elder law attorneys in the United States work in private practice, either in law firms or alone. While it may seem that the best employment possibilities might be found in large cities and metropolitan areas, there is also fierce competition in these places. Many attorneys practice elder law in addition to other areas of law. Additionally, clients often come to their regular attorneys for elder issues that arise in their lives. Since elder law is so client-oriented, the logical approach is to practice where there is a large population of elderly people; therefore, smaller, more rural areas offer numerous opportunities. In addition, the cost of living is lower in these areas, and since the majority of people seeking elder law attorneys are not wealthy and cannot pay astronomical fees, the elder law attorney will find living on a typical income easier in these areas.

STARTING OUT

After graduation from law school, a lawyer's first task is to pass the state bar examination. A new lawyer will often find a job with a law firm, doing research for other lawyers until passing the bar examination and becoming licensed to practice law. Beginning lawyers usually do not go into solo practice right away. It is difficult to become established, and the experience of working beside established lawyers is helpful to the fledgling lawyer. Newly admitted lawyers typically do research and routine work at first. Specialization usually occurs after a lawyer has some experience in general practice, although lawyers at smaller firms might find themselves guided to particular areas earlier. After a few years of successful experience, a lawyer may be ready to go out on his or her own.

Many new lawyers are recruited directly from law school by law firms or other employers. Recruiters come to the law school and interview possible hires. Recent graduates can also get job leads from local and state bar associations.

To start building a practice in elder law, take as many cases that fall into the realm of elder law as you can and become a member of the NAELA. When you have enough experience under your belt and meet the necessary qualifications, become certified as an elder law attorney with the NELF.

ADVANCEMENT

Lawyers with outstanding ability can expect to go a long way in their profession. Beginning lawyers generally start out doing routine research tasks, but as they prove themselves and develop their abilities, opportunities for advancement will arise. They may be promoted to junior partner in a law firm or establish their own practice focused on elder law.

Advancement for elder law attorneys can also take the form of leadership positions in nonprofit organizations that serve to advance education and competence in the field. There are many opportunities to make a contribution to the elderly population by working to support or change the laws and policies that affect senior citizens. In this unique area of legal practice, the potential for reward, although usually not as financially large as other areas of the law, is great.

EARNINGS

Beginning lawyers earn a modest salary, but the potential for higher earnings builds quickly with solid experience. A lawyer just starting out in solo practice may barely make ends meet for the first few years, especially since many law school graduates carry $70,000 to $80,000 in student loan debt. According to the U.S. Department of Labor, the 2009 median salary for practicing lawyers was $113,240, although some senior partners earned well over $1 million a year. Ten percent earned less than $55,270.

According to the National Association for Law Placement, median salaries for new lawyers were $130,000 in 2009, with salaries ranging from \$70,000 to \$160,000 based on the size of the firm. Although salaries for private practice law are attractive, it is important to remember that some lawyers just starting out may struggle for the first few years.

Incomes for elder law attorneys vary greatly but generally are less than those of their colleagues working with wealthy clients, such as corporate lawyers representing major companies.

Benefits and bonuses vary widely in this field. Many attorneys are sole practitioners and therefore don't receive company benefits such as paid vacation, health insurance, and retirement plans. Generally, lawyers who are partners in larger firms may enjoy more generous benefits packages and perks than those with a sole practice.

WORK ENVIRONMENT

Lawyers typically enjoy a pleasant, although busy, work environment. Law offices are usually designed to impress clients and can be quite comfortable. Lawyers may also spend significant time in law libraries or record rooms or in the homes and offices of clients. Courtrooms are usually orderly and efficient workplaces. However, many elder law lawyers never work in a courtroom, and, unless directly involved in litigation, they may never work at a trial.

Working hours for most lawyers are usually regular business hours. Many lawyers, however, have to work long hours when a client's case demands it, spending evenings and weekends preparing cases and materials and working with clients. Besides the time spent working directly on a client's needs, lawyers must always keep up with the latest developments in the profession. Lawyers who work in law firms must often work long hours for senior partners in order to advance in the firm. Spending long weekend hours doing research and interviewing people should be expected.

Elder law attorneys, more than other types of lawyers, can expect to put in more hours visiting their clients in their homes or care facilities, since traveling to the attorney's office may be challenging for some clients. Attorneys who specialize in elder law should be prepared for the realities of life for the elderly, as they are likely to be exposed to various types and stages of illness or infirmity and environments that can be disturbing to some.

OUTLOOK

According to the U.S. Department of Labor, the demand for all lawyers is expected to grow as fast as the average for all occupations through 2018, but those in the specialty of elder law will have the advantage of a rapidly growing elderly population, increasingly complex laws, and unprecedented health care issues. All of these factors combine to make for a substantial client base in need of elder law attorneys. It is estimated that 40 percent of people over 65 will require a nursing home or other long-term care at some point, but few of them have planned financially for that eventuality. People are living longer and encountering a variety of health care problems, many of them debilitating. The sheer numbers of elderly people alone point to a promising future in this career.

However, the outlook is also affected by governmental changes and public policy. It is important to remember that since a majority of elder law clients are seeking legal advice and assistance for Medicare/Medicaid issues, the outlook for the profession is significantly affected by changes in law. If there is a decrease in public benefits, this will affect the workload for elder law attorneys. Additionally, many people do not seek out an elder law attorney in particular for issues such as long-range planning, asset protection, guardianship, and probate practices; rather, they are likely to bring these issues to their regular attorney. In other words, attorneys who may not specialize in elder law often handle a large number of cases involving elder law issues.

The large number of law school graduates each year has created strong competition for jobs, and new attorneys, even those with an eye toward elder law specialization, will initially face stiff competition for jobs.

Lawyers in solo practice will find it hard to earn a living until their practice and reputation are fully established. The best opportunities exist in small towns or suburbs of large cities, where there is less competition and new lawyers can meet potential clients more easily.

FOR MORE INFORMATION

To read member profiles, visit the association's Web site.
  American Association of Trust, Estate and Elder Law Attorneys
  http://www.aateela.org

For information about law student services, approved law schools, and the ABA Commission on Law and Aging, contact
  American Bar Association (ABA)
  321 North Clark Street
  Chicago, IL 60654-7598
  Tel: 800-285-2221
  E-mail: askaba@abanet.org
  http://www.abanet.org and http://new.abanet.org/aging

For information on AALS members, contact
Association of American Law Schools (AALS)
1201 Connecticut Avenue, NW, Suite 800
Washington, DC 20036-2717
Tel: 202-296-8851
E-mail: aals@aals.org
http://www.aals.org

For information on elder law, contact
National Academy of Elder Law Attorneys
1577 Spring Hill Road, Suite 220
Vienna, VA 22182-2223
Tel: 703-942-5711
http://www.naela.org

For information about certification in elder law, contact
National Elder Law Foundation
6336 North Oracle Road, Suite 326, #136
Tucson, AZ 85704-5480
Tel: 520-881-1076
http://www.nelf.org

*For more information on issues affecting the elderly, contact the
following organizations:*
Administration on Aging
Washington, DC 20201-0001
Tel: 202-619-0724
E-mail: aoainfo@aoa.hhs.gov
http://www.aoa.gov

National Institute on Aging
Building 31, Room 5C27
31 Center Drive, MSC 2292
Bethesda, MD 20892-0001
Tel: 301-496-1752
http://www.nia.nih.gov

Financial Planners

QUICK FACTS

School Subjects
Business
Mathematics

Personal Skills
Helping/teaching
Leadership/management

Work Environment
Primarily indoors
Primarily one location

Minimum Education Level
Bachelor's degree

Salary Range
$33,790 to $68,200 to
$215,345+

Certification or Licensing
Recommended (certification)
Required for certain positions (licensing)

Outlook
Much faster than the average

DOT
250

GOE
12.03.01

NOC
1114

O*NET-SOC
13-2052.00, 41-3031.01,
41-3031.02

OVERVIEW

Financial planning is the process of establishing financial goals and creating ways to reach them. Certified *financial planners,* sometimes known as *personal financial advisers,* examine the assets of their clients and suggest what steps they need to take in the future to meet their goals. They take a broad approach to financial advice, which distinguishes them from other professional advisers, such as insurance agents, stockbrokers, accountants, attorneys, and real estate agents, each of whom typically focuses on only one aspect of a person's finances. Approximately 208,400 personal financial advisers are employed in the United States.

HISTORY

Except for the depression years of the 1930s and intermittent recessions, the U.S. economy expanded impressively after World War I. As the average American's income increased, so did lifestyle expectations. By the 21st century, vacations to Disney World, cell phones for everyone in the family, two or three cars in the garage, and thoughts of a financially worry-free retirement were not uncommon. But how do Americans meet such high expectations? More and more have begun turning to professionals—financial planners—who recommend financial strategies. According to a consumer survey done by the Certified Financial Planner Board of Standards (CFP Board), 42 percent of respondents said they had experience with financial planners. In addition, 25 percent were currently using the services of a financial planner. Fee-only planners were the most popular, with 47 percent of respondents noting that they preferred to work with a financial planner who is compensated this way instead of by commission or other means. Fee-only financial planners represent a growing segment of the financial advising industry, but the profession as a whole is booming due to the deregulation of certain institutions dealing with money. Because of this deregulation, banks, brokerage firms, and insurance companies have been allowed to offer more financial services—including investment advice—to customers since 1999. This has created many job openings for planners who want to work for these businesses.

Other reasons for growth in this industry include the large number of people (baby boomers, born between 1945 and 1965) who are closing in on or reaching retirement age and taking stock of their assets. As boomers consider if they have enough money to pay for the retirement they want, more and more of them are turning to financial planners for advice about such things as annuities, long-term health insurance, and individual retirement accounts. Another factor that has spurred growth is the increased awareness people have about investing and other options because of the large amount of financial information now directed at the general public. Today, commercials for brokerage firms, television talk shows with weekly money advice, and financial publications and Web sites all offer various news and tips about what the average person should do with his or her money. All this information can be overwhelming, and people turn to experts for help. According to the CFP Board's survey, 70 percent of respondents felt that financial advisers were a good source of information about financial products. As tax laws change, the world economy becomes more complex, and new technologies alter workforces, financial planners will continue to be in demand for their expert advice.

THE JOB

Financial planners advise their clients on many aspects of finance. Although they seem to be jacks-of-all-trades, certified financial planners do not work alone; they meet with their clients' other advisers, such as attorneys, accountants, trust officers, and investment bankers. Financial planners fully research their clients' overall financial picture. After meeting with the clients and their other advisers, certified financial planners analyze the data they have received and generate a written report that includes their recommendations on how the clients can best achieve their goals. This report details the clients' financial objectives, current income, investments, risk tolerance, expenses, tax returns, insurance coverage, retirement programs, estate plans, and other important information.

Financial planning is an ongoing process. The plan must be monitored and reviewed periodically so that adjustments can be made, if necessary, to assure that it continues to meet individual needs.

The plan itself is a set of recommendations and strategies for clients to use or ignore, and financial planners should be ready to answer hard questions about the integrity of the plans they map out. After all, they are dealing with all of the money and investments that people have worked a lifetime accruing.

People need financial planners for different things. Some might want life insurance, college savings plans, or estate planning. Sometimes these needs are triggered by changes in people's lives, such as retirement, death of a spouse, disability, marriage, birth of children, or job changes. Certified financial planners spend the majority of their time on the following topics: investment planning, retirement planning, tax planning, estate planning, and risk management. All of these areas require different types of financial knowledge, and planners are generally expected to be extremely competent in the disciplines of asset management, employee benefits, estate planning, insurance, investments, and retirement, according to the Certified Financial Planner Board of Standards. A financial planner must also have good interpersonal skills, since establishing solid client–planner relationships is essential to the planner's success. It also helps to have good communication skills, since even the best financial plan, if presented poorly to a client, can be rejected.

Clients drive the job of financial planners. The advice planners provide depends on their clients' particular needs, resources, and priorities. Many people think they cannot afford or do not need a comprehensive financial plan. Certified financial planners must have a certain amount of expertise in sales to build their client base.

Certified financial planners use various ways to develop their client lists, including telephone solicitation, giving seminars on financial planning to the general public or specific organizations, and networking with social contacts. Referrals from satisfied customers also help the business grow.

Although certified financial planners are trained in comprehensive financial planning, some specialize in one area, such as asset management, investments, or retirement planning. In most small or self-owned financial planning companies, they are generalists. However, in some large companies, planners might specialize in particular areas, including insurance, real estate, mutual funds, annuities, pensions, or business valuations.

REQUIREMENTS

High School

If financial planning sounds interesting to you, take as many business classes as possible as well as mathematics. Communication courses, such as speech or drama, will help put you at ease when talking in front of a crowd, something financial planners must do occasionally. English courses will help you prepare the written reports planners present to their clients.

Postsecondary Training

Earning a bachelor's degree starts financial planners on the right track, but it will help if your degree indicates a skill with numbers, be it in science or business. A business administration degree with a specialization in financial planning or a liberal arts degree with courses in accounting, business administration, economics, finance, marketing, human behavior, counseling, and public speaking is excellent preparation for this sort of job.

Certification or Licensing

However, education alone will not motivate clients to turn over their finances to you. Many financial professionals are licensed on the state and federal levels in financial planning specialties, such as stocks and insurance. The Securities and Exchange Commission and most states have licensing requirements for investment advisers, a category under which most financial planners also fall. However, the government does not regulate most of the activities of planners. Therefore, to show credibility to clients, most financial planners choose to become certified as either a certified financial planner (CFP) or a chartered financial consultant (ChFC).

To receive the CFP mark of certification, offered by the CFP Board, candidates must meet what the board refers to as the four E's, which comprise the following.

Education. To be eligible to take the certification exam, candidates must meet education requirements in one of the following ways. The first option is to complete a CFP board-registered program in financial planning. The second is to hold a specific degree and professional credentials in one of several areas the board has approved of; these include certified public accountant, licensed attorney, chartered financial consultant, chartered life underwriter, chartered financial analyst, doctor of business administration, and Ph.D. in business or economics. Lastly, applicants may submit transcripts of their undergraduate or graduate education to the board for review. If the board feels the education requirements have been met, the candidate may sit for the exam. Applicants must also have a bachelor's degree in any area of study or program to obtain CFP certification. They do not need to have earned this degree at the time they take the examination, but must show proof of completion of this degree in order to complete the final stage of certification.

Examination. Once candidates have completed the education requirements, they may take the certification exam, which tests knowledge on various key aspects of financial planning.

Experience. Either before or after passing the certification exam, candidates must have three years of work experience.

Ethics. After candidates have completed the education, examination, and experience requirements, they must voluntarily ascribe to the CFP Board's Code of Ethics and Professional Responsibility and Financial Planning Practice Standards to be allowed to use the CFP mark. This voluntary agreement empowers the board to take action if a CFP licensee violates the code. Such violations could lead to disciplinary action, including permanent revocation of the right to use the CFP mark.

The American College offers the ChFC designation. To receive this designation, candidates must complete certain course work stipulated by The American College, meet experience requirements, and agree to uphold The American College's Code of Ethics and Procedures.

To maintain the CFP and the ChFC designations, professionals will need to meet continuing education and other requirements as determined by the CFP Board and The American College.

Two other organizations offer certification to financial planning professionals. Fi360 (http://www.fi360.com) offers the accredited investment fiduciary and accredited investment fiduciary analyst designations. The Investment Management Consultants Association (http://www.imca.org) offers the following designations: certified investment management analyst and chartered private wealth adviser. Contact these organizations for more information.

Other Requirements

Other factors that contribute to success as a financial planner include keeping up with continuing education, referrals from clients, specialization, people and communication skills, and a strong educational background.

EXPLORING

There is not much that students can do to explore this field, since success as a certified financial planner comes only with training and years on the job. However, you can check out the financial planning information available on the Internet to familiarize yourself with the terms used in the industry. You should also take as many finance and business classes as possible. Talking to certified financial planners will also help you gather information on the field.

EMPLOYERS

Approximately 208,400 personal financial advisers are employed in the United States. Financial planners are employed by financial planning firms across the country. Many of these firms are small, perhaps employing two to 15 people, and most are located in urban areas. A smaller, but growing, number of financial planners are employed by corporations, banks, credit unions, mutual fund companies, insurance companies, accounting or law firms, colleges and universities, credit counseling organizations, and brokerage firms. In addition, many financial planners are self-employed.

STARTING OUT

Early in their careers, financial planners work for banks, mutual fund companies, or investment firms and usually receive extensive on-the-job training. The job will deal heavily with client-based and research activities. Financial planners may start their own business as they learn personal skills and build their client base. During their first few years, certified financial planners spend many hours analyzing documents, meeting with other advisers, and networking to find new clients.

ADVANCEMENT

Those who have not changed their career track in five years can expect to have established some solid, long-term relationships with clients. Measured success at this point will be the planners' service fees, which will be marked up considerably from when they started their careers.

Those who have worked in the industry for 10 years usually have many clients and a six-figure income. Experienced financial planners can also move into careers in investment banking, financial consulting, and financial analysis. Because people skills are also an integral part of being a financial planner, consulting, on both personal and corporate levels, is also an option. Many planners will find themselves attending business school, either to achieve a higher income or to switch to one of the aforementioned professions.

EARNINGS

There are several methods of compensation for financial planners. Fee-only means that compensation is earned entirely from fees from consultation, plan development, or investment management. These fees may be charged on an hourly or project basis depending on clients' needs or on a percentage of assets under management. Commission-only compensation is received from the sale of financial products that clients agree to purchase to implement financial planning recommendations. There is no charge for advice or preparation of the financial plan. Fee-offset means that compensation received in the form of commission from the sale of financial products is offset against fees charged for the planning process. Combination fee/commission is a fee charged for consultation, advice, and financial plan preparation on an hourly, project, or percentage basis. Planners might also receive commissions from recommended products targeted to achieve goals and objectives. Some planners work on a salary basis for financial services institutions such as banks, credit unions, and other related organizations.

The median annual gross income of certified financial planners was $215,345 in 2009, according to the *2009 Survey of Trends in the Financial Planning Industry,* which was conducted by the College for Financial Planning. These incomes were earned from financial plan writing, product sales, consulting, and related activities.

The U.S. Department of Labor reports that financial planners earned a median annual salary of $68,200 in 2009. The most experienced financial planners with the highest level of education earned more than $166,400, while the least experienced financial planners earned less than $33,790.

Firms might also provide beginning financial planners with a steady income by paying a draw, which is a minimum salary based on the commission and fees the planner can be expected to earn.

Some financial planners receive vacation days, sick days, and health insurance, but that depends on whether they work for financial institutions or on their own.

WORK ENVIRONMENT

Most financial planners work by themselves in offices or at home. Others work in offices with other financial planners. Established financial planners usually work the same hours as others in the business community. Beginners who are seeking customers probably work longer hours. Many planners accommodate customers by meeting with them in the evenings and on weekends. They might spend a lot of time out of the office meeting with current and prospective clients, attending civic functions, and participating in trade association meetings.

OUTLOOK

The employment of financial planners is expected to grow by 30 percent through 2018, according to the U.S. Department of Labor— or much faster than the average for all occupations. Employment is expected to grow rapidly in the future for a number of reasons. More funds should be available for investment, as personal income and inherited wealth grow. Demographics will also play a role; as increasing numbers of baby boomers turn 50, demand will grow for retirement-related investments. Most people, in general, are likely to turn to financial planners for assistance with retirement planning. Individual saving and investing for retirement are expected to become more important, as many companies reduce pension benefits and switch from defined-benefit retirement plans to defined-contribution plans, which shift the investment responsibility from the company to the individual. Furthermore, a growing number of individual investors are expected to seek advice from financial planners regarding the increasing complexity and array of investment alternatives for assistance with estate planning.

Due to the highly competitive nature of financial planning, many beginners leave the field because they are not able to establish a sufficient clientele. Once established, however, planners have a strong attachment to their occupation because of high earning potential and considerable investment in training. Job opportunities should be best for mature individuals with successful work experience.

FOR MORE INFORMATION

For more information about financial education and the ChFC designation, contact

The American College
270 South Bryn Mawr Avenue
Bryn Mawr, PA 19010-2105
Tel: 888-263-7265
E-mail: professionaleducation@theamericancollege.edu
http://www.theamericancollege.edu

To learn more about financial planning and to obtain a copy of the Guide to CFP Certification, *contact*

Certified Financial Planner Board of Standards
1425 K Street, NW, Suite 500
Washington, DC 20005-3686
Tel: 800-487-1497
E-mail: mail@CFPBoard.org
http://www.cfp.net

For information on financial planning, visit the FPA Web site.
Financial Planning Association (FPA)
4100 East Mississippi Avenue, Suite 400
Denver, CO 80246-3053
Tel: 800-322-4237
http://www.fpanet.org

For more information on fee-only financial advisers, contact
National Association of Personal Financial Advisors
3250 North Arlington Heights Road, Suite 109
Arlington Heights, IL 60004-1574
Tel: 847-483-5400
E-mail: info@napfa.org
http://www.napfa.org

Geriatric care managers perform tasks that are similar to some done by social workers, counselors, advocates, and family members. Their duties, depending on the individual, can include providing full-scale assessments of a client's needs, seeing to it that their clients take their medications and make it to scheduled doctors' appointments, taking clients grocery shopping, and providing other family members with written reports detailing how the client is doing. Mainly, though, their role is that of a coordinator. Care managers understand the health care system as well as know about services, such as Meals on Wheels or dog walking, social activities for seniors, and other such resources in their area. It is their job to put clients in touch with the services that they need.

A geriatric care manager's day might include time spent on the phone arranging services for a client; touching base with a client's family members; assisting a client with making a move from a current home to one that provides a higher level of care; conducting an assessment of a new client to determine his or her needs; talking with a bank trust officer about a client's increased care needs; accompanying a client on a trip to the emergency room; or monitoring plans and services. One of a care manager's most important tasks is to help simplify and explain options to clients and assist them and their families in making informed decisions about their health management.

Many geriatric care managers are called upon by family members who live at too great a distance to continue to assist and care for their parents. Known as the "sandwich generation," these adults are struggling to both raise their children and take care of their aging parents. These are often two-career couples and neither the wife nor the husband can leave their work on a regular basis or for long periods to take care of an elderly parent's needs, such as going to the dentist one day and an optometrist appointment the next. In these circumstances, a trusted, reliable professional who assists in taking care of the elderly person's needs can make a big difference in quality of life, for both the elderly person and the other family members.

One of geriatric care managers' most valuable attributes is that they are educated, experienced, informed resources who understand the range of services available and have the knowledge and savvy to navigate any red tape involved. They are able to assess a client's medical needs, mental health, financial situation, legal needs, medications, physical limitations, and family and community support. They are experts in the wide range of services available to the elderly, and they recommend services based upon each client's means and needs. They find assistance that meets the client's needs but does not exceed their resources, financially, emotionally, or physically. In so doing, geriatric care managers not only help contain expenses

Books to Read

Cress, Cathy Jo. *Care Managers: Working With the Aging Family.* Sudbury, Mass.: Jones & Bartlett Publishers, 2008.

Cress, Cathy Jo. *Handbook of Geriatric Care Management.* 2d ed. Sudbury, Mass.: Jones & Bartlett Publishers, 2007.

Mullahy, Catherine. *The Case Manager's Handbook.* 4th ed. Sudbury, Mass.: Jones & Bartlett Publishers, 2009.

Robnett, Regula H., and Walter C. Chop. *Gerontology for the Health Care Professional.* 2d ed. Sudbury, Mass.: Jones & Bartlett Publishers, 2009.

for their clients but also help ensure the elderly person remains as independent as possible.

Usually, care managers get new clients when a family is faced with a crisis involving an elderly member and seeks out help. While it's not preferable to make decisions in emotionally charged situations, a crisis is often the impetus that spurs a family into action. Often this situation is complicated because the family feels that some kind of intervention is needed, but the elderly person might feel everything is fine and not want help.

Many times families on tight budgets have simple needs in mind when they contact a care manager. For example, they might call on a geriatric care manager to help an elderly member take care of tasks such as getting the house painted or taking a pet to the veterinarian. Such help allows the older person to remain at home for as long as possible, which is a financial advantage as well as a lifestyle preference. Such an arrangement also provides peace of mind to other family members.

Geriatric care managers must also do a lot of paperwork, keeping up-to-date files on their clients, scheduling meetings, and writing reports to families. And since many care managers are in business for themselves, they must also do a number of administrative tasks. These tasks include recordkeeping for the business, billing clients, managing the business's finances, and doing advertising or marketing work to attract new clients. Clearly, the geriatric care manager must be comfortable taking on many responsibilities.

The significance of this job should not be underestimated. Geriatric care managers hold positions of great importance, and their work benefits society, the elderly, and the families involved. It should be noted that this work can take an emotional toll, as care managers must deal with their feelings about the inevitable decline and death of their clients. Nevertheless, many find this a rewarding career, knowing that they are working to improve the lives of the elderly.

REQUIREMENTS

High School

You should take a college preparatory curriculum, and, because many skills are necessary to be an effective geriatric care manager, there are plenty of classes you can take to help prepare you for this work. Classes in health are an obvious choice; geriatric care managers need to have an understanding of the human body and how its functions are affected by the aging process. Psychology courses are helpful, since you will need to understand and deal with a variety of people in a myriad of circumstances. Courses in sociology can introduce you to yet another aspect of the geriatric and health care realm. Sciences, such as biology and chemistry, are also useful. Don't neglect your math studies, since you may need to deal with clients' financial questions as well as keep your own records regarding billing and expenses. You will also benefit from English or communication courses, as it will be imperative that you can convey information effectively to your clients and their families.

Postsecondary Training

There are a number of career paths you can take to enter this field. Geriatric care managers usually have a minimum of a bachelor's degree in a field such as nursing, psychology, gerontology, or social work, and many also have master's degrees. While you are in college, therefore, you should consider majoring in one of these subjects, and the courses you take will fulfill the requirements for that major. Those interested in nursing may take classes such as human growth and development, pathophysiology, and pharmacotherapeutics, for example, while those pursuing a bachelor's degree in social work may take classes in social welfare policies, human behavior and social environments, and a field practicum. In addition, take any courses that focus on the elderly in order to get an understanding of their needs and situations. Some people begin working after college with the goal of becoming involved with elderly clients to gain experience before setting up their own care management business. In some cases, local geriatric care management services may offer internships, and this may be another way to gain experience.

Those who go on to get master's degrees will take advanced courses in their field of interest. For example, nurses in master's programs focusing on gerontology may take classes such as older adults in primary care, advanced health assessment, and medical legal issues; those in master's programs in social work may take courses such as sociobehavioral theory and social work methods; and so forth. Like people with bachelor's degrees, those with master's degrees may begin working at a job in their general field (nursing, psychology, social work, etc.) while trying to get as much exposure to geriatric clientele as they can. This allows them to gain experience and make contacts before they begin their independent careers as geriatric care managers.

Certification or Licensing
The National Academy of Certified Care Managers has been administering a certification program since 1997. Those who meet education and experience requirements and pass a written test receive the designation care manager, certified. Other certifications are offered by the Commission for Case Manager Certification (http://www.ccmcertification.org) and the National Association of Social Workers (http://www.socialworkers.org/credentials). Currently, no licensing exists for geriatric care managers as such. Those who have a background in a field requiring licensing, such as nursing, social work, or psychology, are licensed in that field.

Other Requirements
Geriatric care management is a field that requires a lot of the so-called soft skills; compassion, responsibility, patience, and ethics are some of the more obvious characteristics. Assertiveness is also important, as you will be acting as an advocate for your clients, going to whatever lengths necessary to get your client what he or she needs and deserves. A professional demeanor is important, as you will be dealing with attorneys, trust officers, care providers, and other professionals, as well as the client's concerned family members or friends. Good judgment and assessment skills are a necessity. You should also have extensive knowledge of health care issues and the resources that are available to your clients. You will need to maintain a calm disposition in a crisis. You might find yourself accompanying a client to the emergency room, comforting family members during bad times, or visiting clients in what can be disturbing environments. You should be a people person, able to form long-term relationships with clients and their families, because your role will be one of great importance to them.

EXPLORING
You might find it informative to talk to your parents about the current and future needs of older relatives. These matters are best

Words to Know

adult day care center: center featuring structured programs, usually during weekdays, that may include activities, meals, and health and rehabilitative services for the elderly in a supervised setting; transportation is sometimes included in the fee

assisted living: facility that provides individual living units, which may or may not have a kitchenette; the facility offers 24-hour, on-site response staff; additional nursing or home care services can be provided at an additional fee

companion: provides assistance with shopping, meal preparation, escort, companionship, and home upkeep; no personal care or nursing care is provided

conservator: person appointed by the court in a legal proceeding to act as the legal representative of a person who is mentally or physically incapable of managing his or her own affairs

emergency response systems: allows for 24-hour monitoring and response to medical or other emergencies

guardianship: similar to a conservatorship yet severely restricts the legal rights of an elder based on a court's finding of legal incompetence

home health care agency: agency providing medical care in the home; services can include nursing; occupational, speech, or physical therapy; social work; or a home health aide; Medicare usually only covers this care during an acute period of illness

long-term care insurance: privately paid policy that provides money for predetermined health care costs after policyholder meets certain medical requirements

Medicaid/medical assistance: federal and state government program in which the states provide health care for low-income people

Medicare: federal program providing health care coverage/insurance for people over 65 and some people with disabilities; Part A covers in-patient care, skilled nursing facility, hospice, and short-term health care; Part B covers doctors' services, outpatient hospital care, and durable medical equipment; does not provide for long-term care of the elderly except under limited conditions

power of attorney: legal document allowing one person to act in a legal matter on another's behalf

respite: time off designed to relieve the caregiver from caregiving duties either in the home, community setting, or care facility

approached with some sensitivity, as you may encounter reluctance to discuss the topic. Being able to extend empathy and compassion is another key characteristic of a successful geriatric care manager, so this is an important area to explore.

It is always valuable to talk to an experienced professional in the field you are considering. Your high school counselor, a local business directory, or the National Association of Professional Geriatric Care Managers may be able to provide you with leads in locating a geriatric care manager who would be willing to talk with you about the job. (See the end of this article for contact information.)

You may also find value in speaking to professionals in related fields, such as lawyers in elder law, nurses and doctors in geriatric medicine, managers of nursing homes, physical therapists, and so forth.

An excellent way to explore this field is to volunteer at a geriatric program or facility. Working with the elderly can be very rewarding, and you will have the opportunity to talk directly with many older people. Being able to relate to those of a different generation is a key skill of this job.

You can also volunteer at a nursing home or extended care facility. This work can be more challenging, but it will provide you with an opportunity to discover your ability to work with those with failing mental and physical capacities in the context of their living environment.

EMPLOYERS

The majority of geriatric care managers are employed in private practice. Others are employed by elder care service organizations, adult day care centers, elder abuse programs, banks, and other institutions or businesses that have dealings with older people. Some faith-based agencies, such as CJE SeniorLife (formerly Council for Jewish Elderly), also offer geriatric care management. Any of these might be potential employers; even individual practitioners may be likely to hire assistants and caregiving aides.

Health maintenance organizations do not currently pay for geriatric care management services. As the population ages and the collective voice of senior citizens grows louder, we may see more subsidized care management for the elderly. Managed care organizations are beginning to recognize that geriatric care managers play a key role in cost control. Geriatric care managers' services in promoting their clients' health, safety, and overall well-being save managed care organizations money by lowering the occurrence of such things as small illnesses, which, left untreated, become major illnesses requiring hospitalizations.

Geriatric care managers can work in numerous places across the country. Many jobs will be clustered around major metropolitan areas, but opportunities will exist virtually anywhere.

STARTING OUT

One method of becoming a geriatric care manager is to work in a related field, such as social work, nursing, or nursing home management, before moving on to a care manager career. Jobs in these areas will give you experience and allow you to interact with those who are already geriatric care managers. In this way you can build up your resume, make connections at various agencies, learn about local resources, and perhaps even begin establishing a clientele for your own business as a geriatric care manager.

Another possibility is to start out working for another care manager who is already established in the field. This will allow you to learn the job at your own pace and gradually step up to the full duties of the position. You will have the opportunity to provide services to existing clients within the limits of your abilities. As you learn and grow, the geriatric care manager may allow you to take on more and more of the duties of your intended career. In this way you will also gain experience and make contacts that will ultimately help you develop your own clientele.

A third option is to work with your school's career services office, which may have job listings or receive notices from agencies about openings. In addition, consider joining a professional organization, such as the National Association of Professional Geriatric Care Managers. This will help you keep up to date on topics important to those working with the elderly and give you an excellent opportunity to network with professionals.

ADVANCEMENT

Advancement options depend to a large extent on each geriatric care manager's goals. For example, those who work as assistants to other care managers or those who are part of a business with several care managers may want to advance by starting their own management service. Those with their own care management services may advance by establishing an excellent reputation and increasing their clientele. A sizeable client base, in turn, will boost the business's earnings; additionally, the care managers may then raise their fees for their in-demand services. On the other hand, some geriatric care managers who have their own businesses may consider it an advancement to form a partnership with other care managers. One benefit of this would be that each manager could concentrate on the areas of care management he or she enjoys the most. Another possibility is for a geriatric care manager in solo private practice to move to a different work setting; for example, a manager may leave solo practice to work for an organization, such as a faith-based group, that provides geriatric care management. And, naturally, this situation could be reversed: a manager could move from a job with an organization to a job in private practice.

No matter what route to advancement geriatric care managers choose, the key factors to their success will be having a reputation for doing excellent work, keeping their knowledge about laws, finances, medications, and services up to date, and enjoying working with and for the elderly.

EARNINGS

Earnings in this field vary widely with experience and geographical location. Those who are in private practice tend to charge an hourly rate. This rate can vary depending, again, on the manager's location (small town, big city, East Coast, Midwest, etc.), the manager's experience and education (those with master's degrees and several years of experience are typically able to charge higher rates), and the service the manager is providing. A 2010 salary survey by Payscale.com reported earnings for geriatric care managers as ranging from $38,884 to $61,445, depending on level of experience.

Someone just starting out in private practice may have a small number of clients and only manage to bill for 15 or 20 hours a week. Naturally, a manager's workload will directly affect earnings; the more hours a manager can bill for, the higher the annual earnings.

The U.S. Department of Labor reports that health services managers who worked in the field of home health care (a related occupation) earned mean annual salaries of $83,160 in 2009.

A typical client will require an initial period of more intense activity on the manager's part to assess his or her needs and set up services. This will often be a crisis-driven event, possibly requiring last-minute travel and other arrangements. Following this, the client will typically require less of a care manager's time each month to maintain services and periodically reassess needs.

A majority of geriatric care managers must provide their own benefits, as so many are self-employed. Those who work for larger organizations might earn lower wages than independent consultants, but they will likely have a range of benefits such as health insurance, vacation and sick days, and retirement plans.

WORK ENVIRONMENT

Geriatric care managers spend a significant amount of time with their clients, both in their homes and in nursing facilities. The quality of these environments can range from pleasant to disturbing, depending on the condition of the client. Typically, however, managers work in quiet, indoor environments. Managers frequently need to communicate with other professionals while coordinating a client's medical, legal, and everyday needs, so much telephone work is involved. Depending on the size or the business or organization, managers may supervise and help out with the work of others. Schedules may be quite busy one day with unexpected emergencies, such as a client falling and going to the hospital, and quiet the next day with recordkeeping, phone calls, and paperwork. Many geriatric care managers are on call, available to their clients at all times for sudden needs.

This line of work can be emotionally challenging. A successful geriatric care manager will need to be able to handle anger, grief, frustration, and confusion. Conflict and stress can also occur, as care managers have to defend the rights of their clients, sometimes against the wishes of the clients' families and friends.

OUTLOOK

Geriatric care management is a fairly new profession, and, as such, the U.S. Department of Labor does not have specific employment outlook information for geriatric care managers. However, the more general category of human service worker is expected to grow much faster than the average for all occupations through 2018, according to the U.S. Department of Labor. Job opportunities in the field of geriatric care management are excellent, especially for those with advanced education.

In many aspects, this job represents the replacement of a traditional family function, that of caring for the elderly. As people live longer, as families typically become geographically separated, and as health insurance becomes more complicated, the need for geriatric care managers has grown dramatically. Experts predict this need only to grow in the next decade.

FOR MORE INFORMATION

This government agency has press releases, resources for students of gerontology, and news for family caregivers. For information, contact
   Administration on Aging
   Washington, DC 20201-0001
   Tel: 202-619-0724
   E-mail: aoainfo@aoa.hhs.gov
   http://www.aoa.gov

For information on continuing education programs, job listings, and student resources, check out the following Web site:
   American Society on Aging
   71 Stevenson Street, Suite 1450
   San Francisco, CA 94105-2938
   Tel: 415-974-9600
   E-mail: info@asaging.org
   http://www.asaging.org

AGHE, a section of the Gerontological Society of America, promotes education in the field of aging and offers a directory of gerontology and geriatrics programs.
   Association for Gerontology in Higher Education (AGHE)
   1220 L Street, NW, Suite 901
   Washington, DC 20005-4018
   Tel: 202-289-9806
   http://www.aghe.org

For information about certification, contact
   National Academy of Certified Care Managers
   PO Box 669
   244 Upton Road
   Colchester, CT 06415-0669
   Tel: 800-962-2260
   E-mail: naccm@snet.net
   http://www.naccm.net

For information for both family and professional caregivers, contact
   National Alliance for Caregiving
   4720 Montgomery Lane, 2nd Floor
   Bethesda, MD 20814-5320
   E-mail: info@caregiving.org
   http://www.caregiving.org

For career information, contact
National Association of Professional Geriatric Care Managers
3275 West Ina Road, Suite 130
Tucson, AZ 85741-2198
Tel: 520-881-8008
http://www.caremanager.org

For a wealth of information about topics relevant to seniors, contact
National Council on Aging
1901 L Street, NW, 4th Floor
Washington, DC 20036-3540
Tel: 202-479-1200
http://www.ncoa.org

For news releases, reports, and information on geriatric care, contact
National Institute on Aging
Building 31, Room 5C27
31 Center Drive, MSC 2292
Bethesda, MD 20892-0001
Tel: 301-496-1752
http://www.nia.nih.gov

INTERVIEW

Chris Austin is a certified professional geriatric care manager and licensed social worker and the owner of My Life, LLC Geriatric Care Management in Eagan, Minnesota. She discussed her career with the editors of Careers in Focus: Geriatric Care.

Q. Please tell us a little about yourself. What made you want to become a geriatric care manager?

A. I am a licensed social worker by trade. I began my social work career about 10 years ago as a mental health case manager. In that capacity I worked in the community providing case management services to adults who had serious and persistent mental illness, many of whom were senior citizens. I eventually began working with elderly individuals in long-term care settings. Over the years, I have worked as a social worker in hospitals, nursing homes, transitional care units, and community settings. About three years ago, I completed a graduate program in business. Following graduate school, I worked as a director in a nursing home and hospital. My hands-on work in social services provided me with skills in care management, and my most recent jobs in leadership have helped me to develop the skills needed to start my own business and work independently. Though a master's degree or experience in business is not required to be a geriatric care manager, it can be a valuable asset to those geriatric care managers who are interested in working independently. This is a very common business model for many care managers. I greatly enjoy the satisfaction that comes from helping others, particularly senior citizens and their families. I also enjoy the satisfaction of being my own boss.

Q. Can you please describe a day in your life on the job?

A. Geriatric care mangers provide supportive services for elderly individuals and their families. They also develop plans to anticipate a client's future needs, and address crisis situations. Most days include a visit to an elderly person in their home. The purpose of the visit may be to check in on the client and ensure that they are receiving the appropriate amount of services to meet their current needs. When a client is new to a care manager, the care manager will spend time with the client in their home environment and conduct assessments to determine their current level of functioning. Care managers are trained to assess a client's mental, emotional, social, medical, financial, dietary, and cognitive status. They then coordinate necessary services based on identified needs. This work may be conducted in the client's home or at the care manager's office. Care managers may also accompany clients to medical appointments, care conferences, or tour alternative living settings. When a crisis arises, care managers must be available to address immediate issues, even if it is in the middle of the night. This may require meeting a client in a hospital emergency room.

Q. What are the most important personal and professional qualities for geriatric care managers?

A. Geriatric care managers usually have a degree in a human service related field, such as social work, nursing, occupational therapy, or gerontology. The National Association of Professional Geriatric Care Managers is a nationally recognized trade association that certifies care managers. To become certified, a care manager must have a college degree in a human service-related field, and must have work experience both in case management and work with elderly individuals. Because much of a care manager's work is done in the client's home or in the community, care managers must be able to work independently.

Geriatric care managers must have a passion for helping elderly individuals and their families, and must be able to problem solve complex issues. Care managers must also possess good communication and follow-up skills.

Q. What are some of the pros and cons of your job?

A. Work as a geriatric care manger can oftentimes be very rewarding. Most clients and their families will form a close working relationship with their care manager. Geriatric care managers are often considered to be an extended family member. This can be very satisfying work for the professional who enjoys working closely with people and helping others. Geriatric care managers spend most of their day out of the office. This means they must do a lot of driving and spend time in transit. Sometimes, geriatric care managers are hired to help diffuse difficult family dynamics, or sort through a medical crisis. Care managers may feel "caught in the middle," or may have to navigate clients through negative emotions such as anger, fear, anxiety, and grief. This can be exhausting and even cause burnout if the care manager is not careful about separating work from leisure time.

Q. What is the future employment outlook for geriatric care managers?

A. According to some statistics, it is estimated that the number of persons age 65 and older will increase by 225 percent between the years 2015 and 2030. Additionally, federal, state, and local budget shortfalls have created complexities within health care systems. There is a great deal of speculation that there will not be enough health care workers to support the aging baby boomers, and gaining access to appropriate senior services will be an overwhelming and daunting task. Thus, there will continue to be a growing need for geriatric care managers who can help seniors and their families navigate complex systems and locate adequate and appropriate services. However, economic conditions may play a role in the degree to which our current seniors are willing to pay privately for geriatric care management services. Because many senior citizens have experienced a significant decrease in the assets that they once had due to stock market devaluations, individuals needing services cannot justify paying for them. Additionally, many adult children are finding themselves out of work, and have moved back home with their aging parents. Because of this, family members are assuming an informal role of caretaker, and sometimes, care manager. This has ultimately had an impact on the demand for geriatric care management services. Fortunately, as national economic conditions improve, care management services will be in greater demand.

Q. What advice would you give to young people who want to enter the field?

A. While a formal, four-year education is required to become a certified geriatric care manager, the most important attribute one must posses is industry knowledge gained through work experience. A person interested in becoming a geriatric care manager can gain experience by volunteering and working in a variety of different capacities within the senior care industry. Local senior centers, senior living communities, nursing homes, and hospitals offer many volunteer opportunities. Students who are interested in pursuing a nursing degree can gain entry-level employment as a nursing assistant in nursing homes and other senior residential settings. This will give the student working experience as well as exposure to the senior population. Spending as much time as possible with elderly adults, particularly those suffering from memory loss, can be a valuable experience that creates a great foundation for geriatric care management.

Geriatricians

OVERVIEW

A *geriatrician* is a physician with specialized knowledge in the prevention, diagnosis, treatment, and rehabilitation of disorders common to old age. The term *geriatrics* refers to the clinical aspects of aging and the comprehensive health care of older people. It is an area of medicine that focuses on health and disease in old age and is a growing medical specialty.

HISTORY

Geriatricians specialize in working with the elderly. The term geriatrics comes from the Greek terms, *geras*, meaning old age, and *iatrikos*, meaning physician. Geriatrics has only fairly recently become a popular, necessary, and recognized specialty. Formal training in the field is relatively new. One reason for the development of this occupation is that people are now living longer. According to the U.S. Census Bureau, there were three million Americans age 65 or over living in 1900, but by 2000 this segment of the population had grown to about 35 million. This large (and growing) number of older people has created a demand for specialized services. Geriatricians are doctors who fulfill this demand. As our elderly population continues to grow—the bureau predicts approximately 82 million people to be age 65 or over by 2050—geriatricians are faced with unique medical and ethical challenges in the treatment of their patients.

THE JOB

Geriatricians spend most of their time with patients, taking patient histories, listening to their comments or symptoms, and running any of a number of diagnostic tests and evaluations, including physical examinations. Geriatricians generally see patients in a clinic, a long-term care facility, or a hospital. Each patient setting requires a unique type of patient care. Geriatricians often work with other physicians to diagnose and treat multiple problems and to provide the best possible care for each patient.

For example, an elderly man's complaint of fatigue could signal one or more of a large number of disorders. Diagnosis may be complicated by the coexistence of physical and mental problems, such as heart disease and dementia (mental confusion). This may mean consulting with a psychiatrist to treat the dementia and a cardiologist for the heart problems. Not only do geriatricians work with other medical personnel, they also work with family members and community services. Very often geriatricians work with the patient's family in order to get an accurate diagnosis, proper care, and follow-up treatment. If the patient is living alone, the geriatrician might also need the support of a social worker, neighbor, or relative to make certain that proper medication is administered and that the patient is monitored. If there is no cure for the patient's condition, the geriatrician must devise some way of helping the patient cope with the condition.

Paperwork is also a large part of geriatricians' jobs, as they must complete forms, sign releases, write prescriptions, and meet the requirements of Medicare and private insurance companies.

REQUIREMENTS

High School

To become a doctor, you will need to devote many years to schooling before you are admitted to practice. Your first step, therefore, should be to take a college preparatory curriculum while in high school. Take four years of math, English, and science classes. Biology, chemistry, and physics are particularly important to take. Study a foreign language and, if your high school offers it, the language you take should be Latin. Many medical terms you will encounter later on have roots in the Latin language. In addition, round out your education with history courses and courses such as psychology and sociology, which may give you a greater understanding of people, an asset in this people-oriented career.

A geriatrician provides encouragement to a 90-year-old patient in a nursing home. *(Steve Helber, AP Photo)*

Postsecondary Training

To become a geriatrician, you will need to earn a college degree and a medical degree, complete specialized training, and become licensed. After students have completed this phase of their education, they get more training through a residency, with study in a specialty area. Geriatric care is generally considered a subspecialty. So students complete their residency in one specialty area, such as internal medicine, and then go on to complete a fellowship in geriatric care. The length of these programs varies, and they can take anywhere from one to four years to complete. The Association for Gerontology in Higher Education publishes the *Directory of Educational Programs in Gerontology and Geriatrics,* which has information on educational programs available at various levels, including fellowship programs.

Certification or Licensing

A certificate of added qualifications in geriatric medicine or geriatric psychiatry is offered through the certifying boards in family practice, internal medicine, osteopathic medicine, and psychiatry for physicians who have completed a fellowship program in geriatrics. The American Board of Internal Medicine is just one of many professional medical boards that provide certification to qualified geriatricians.

In addition, all physicians must be licensed to practice. After receiving their medical degree, new physicians are required to take a licensing examination conducted through the board of medical examiners in each state. Some states have reciprocity agreements with other states so that a physician licensed in one state may be automatically licensed in another without being required to pass another examination. Because this is not true throughout the United States, however, the wise physician will find out about licensing procedures before planning to move.

Other Requirements
The career of a geriatrician is both intellectually and emotionally demanding. A good geriatrician needs to be able to effectively manage all aspects of a patient's problems, including social and emotional issues. Thus, creative problem-solving skills are an asset. Geriatricians must have a general interest in aging and the problems related to growing older. They should be effective communicators and listeners and be able to work well as members of a team. And, like any doctor, geriatricians must be committed to lifelong learning, because new advances in medicine occur continuously.

EXPLORING
You can start exploring this field by reading as much as you can about the profession. Remember to visit Web sites of professional organizations for more career-related information. Ask your high school counselor or a science teacher to arrange for a career day in which a doctor from the local community can come in and speak to your class about the work. You can also talk with your family physician to find out what medical school and the work in general is like.

One of the best introductions to a career in health care is to volunteer at a local hospital, clinic, or nursing home. In this way, it is possible to get a feel for what it's like to work around other health care professionals and patients. In some settings, such as nursing homes, you will also find out how well you like working with older people. Other volunteer opportunities exist to work with older people as well. Check with local agencies for seniors to see if there are any outreach programs you can join. In this way you'll have direct contact with the elderly. For example, you may be asked to become a "buddy" and visit with a senior on a regular basis. Again, this will help you determine how much you enjoy being around older people as well as give you the chance to discover what they have to offer.

EMPLOYERS

Geriatricians can find employment in a wide variety of settings, including hospitals, nursing homes, long-term care facilities, and managed-care offices. Some are self-employed in their own or group practices.

Geriatricians interested in teaching work at medical schools or university hospitals. There are also positions available in government agencies such as the National Institutes of Health and the Department of Veterans Affairs. Pharmaceutical companies and chemical companies are also potential employers. They may hire geriatricians to help research and develop new drugs, instruments, and procedures.

STARTING OUT

There are no shortcuts to entering the medical profession. You will need to complete all the required schooling and training and become licensed before you are ready to enter practice. When starting out, some doctors choose to open a private practice or join an established practice. Others take jobs with hospitals and managed-care facilities. Positions are also available with government agencies, such as the National Institute on Aging. Because the education period for physicians is so long, they have the time and opportunities to make many contacts in the field. These contacts are often useful when a doctor looks for employment. Doctors may also use the services of specialized job placement agencies that work only with physicians or that work only with health care professionals of all types.

ADVANCEMENT

Advancement will depend to a large extent on a geriatrician's personal interests and goals. Some with experience may become medical directors of long-term care facilities or the heads of geriatrics divisions of HMOs. Those who are interested in teaching can advance through the ranks to hold full professorships. Geriatricians in private practice can advance with time and experience by building up their client base and creating a large practice. Other possibilities include moving into administration to direct nursing homes, home care programs, or chronic care facilities.

EARNINGS

First-year medical interns earned $47,458 in 2009, according to the Association of American Medical Colleges. According to a salary survey conducted by the recruiting agency Physicians Search, starting salaries for those in internal medicine range from approximately $95,000 to $145,000. The average salary for those specializing in internal medicine was $166,400 in 2009, according to the U.S. Department of Labor. Top salaries of $200,000 or more are not uncommon in this profession. Although these are not figures specifically for geriatricians, they are comparable to what these specialists earn. Earnings are also affected by what area of the country a physician works in, type of employer, size of the practice, and even his or her reputation.

Benefits depend on the employer, but usually include standard ones such as vacation time and insurance. Self-employed geriatricians must provide their own benefits.

WORK ENVIRONMENT

Work environments are influenced by the setting in which geriatricians work—that is, hospitals, private offices, nursing homes, or schools, for example. Any geriatrician who works with patients, however, will practice in offices and examining rooms that are well equipped, clean, attractive, well lighted, and well ventilated. Geriatricians in private practice usually see patients by appointments that are scheduled according to individual requirements. In private offices there is usually at least one nurse-receptionist, and there may be several nurses, a laboratory technician, one or more secretaries, and a bookkeeper.

Because treating an older patient can be very complicated, geriatricians usually find that they have a lot of interaction with other doctors and health care professionals as they work out treatment plans.

Geriatricians working at medical schools or doing research will also find themselves in clean, well-equipped environments. Paperwork will be part of any geriatrician's job. It may range from documenting research to completing insurance forms to filling out grade reports. The environment in any of these settings will be professional.

OUTLOOK

Employment for all physicians is expected to grow much faster than the average for all careers through 2018. The outlook should be even better for those working in geriatric medicine. As the large generation of baby boomers ages, more physicians will be needed to treat their specific needs. Only a small number of physicians each year decide to work in geriatrics. The American Geriatrics Society reports that there is presently a shortage of geriatricians. There is currently only one geriatrician for every 5,000 adults who are age 65 and older. If expected shortages continue, there will only be one geriatrician for every 7,665 older adults by 2030—which suggests that employment opportunities will be especially strong for workers in this field.

FOR MORE INFORMATION

For information on geriatric psychiatry, contact
American Association for Geriatric Psychiatry
7910 Woodmont Avenue, Suite 1050
Bethesda, MD 20814-3004
Tel: 301-654-7850
E-mail: main@aagponline.org
http://www.aagpgpa.org

For information on board certification, contact
American Board of Family Medicine
1648 McGrathiana Parkway, Suite 550
Lexington, KY 40511-1247
Tel: 888-995-5700
E-mail: help@theabfm.org
https://www.theabfm.org

For general information on geriatric care, contact
The American Geriatrics Society
350 Fifth Avenue, Suite 801
New York, NY 10118-0801
Tel: 212-308-1414
E-mail: info@americangeriatrics.org
http://www.americangeriatrics.org

For information on careers in aging, visit the following Web site:
Association for Gerontology in Higher Education
1220 L Street, NW, Suite 901
Washington, DC 20005-4018
Tel: 202-289-9806
http://www.aghe.org

Visit the following Web site for detailed information about careers in gerontology:
Careers in Aging: Resources for Developing Your Career in Aging
http://www.aghe.org/templates/System/detailsasp?id=40634&
PID=500215

Geriatric Nurses

OVERVIEW

Geriatric nurses provide direct patient care to elderly people in their homes, or in hospitals, nursing homes, and clinics. The term *geriatrics* refers to the clinical aspects of aging and the overall health care of the aging population. Since older people tend to have different reactions to illness and disease than younger people, treating them has become a specialty.

HISTORY

The specialty of gerontology nursing started developing in the 20th century as people routinely began to live longer than in past generations. Healthier lifestyles, new medicines, and new medical procedures, among other things, contributed to this change in life span. And as more and more people lived longer, a growing number needed and wanted the expertise of health care professionals who are well versed in the needs and concerns of older people. Geriatric nurses are able to address the special health problems older people may face, such as serious chronic problems (heart disease or blood pressure illness), decreases in senses and physical agility (sight, hearing, balance) that lead to injuries from accidents, and the problems that may result from accidents (learning to walk again after a broken hip). They also care for patients in hospice programs who are in the final stages of a terminal illness.

The Administration on Aging reports that in 2000, the senior population (those 65 and over) was approximately 35 million. This figure is expected to rise steadily and the number of seniors living in

2030 will be approximately 71.5 million. Thus, health care services for seniors will continue to be a growing field.

THE JOB

Geriatric nurses focus primarily on caring for elderly patients. This care may be provided in an institution, in the home as a visiting nurse or hospice nurse, in a retirement community, in a doctor's office, in the hospital, or at wellness clinics in the community. Some geriatric nurses may also give health seminars or workshops to the elderly in the community, or they may be involved in research or pilot studies that deal with health and disease among the aging population.

Geriatric nurses can expect to perform many of the skills required of any nursing professional. Many nurses who specialize in other types of care, with the exception of pediatrics and obstetrics, almost always find themselves caring for the elderly as well.

There are many nursing specialties under the broad umbrella of geriatric nursing. The following paragraphs describe a few of them.

Home health care nurses, also called *visiting nurses,* provide home-based health care under the direction of a physician. They care for persons who may be recovering from an accident, illness, surgery, cancer, or childbirth. They may work for a community organization, a private health care provider, or they may be independent nurses who work on a contract basis.

While home health care nurses care for patients expecting to recover, *hospice nurses* care for people who are in the final stages of a terminal illness. Typically, a hospice patient has less than six months to live. Hospice nurses provide medical and emotional support to the patients and their families and friends. Hospice care usually takes place in the patient's home, but patients may also receive hospice care in a hospital room, nursing home, or a relative's home.

Medications nurses have additional pharmacology training. They have an extensive knowledge of drugs and their effects on the elderly, and oversee the administration of medications to patients. Many state and federal laws now dictate how facilities can restrain their patients either physically or medicinally, so the medications nurse must be aware of these laws and see that the facility abides by these rules.

Another type of geriatric nurse is a *charge nurse,* who oversees a particular shift of nurses and aides who care for the elderly. Although all health providers are required to do a lot of paperwork to document the care they provide and patients' progress, the charge nurse and administrators are responsible for even more documen-

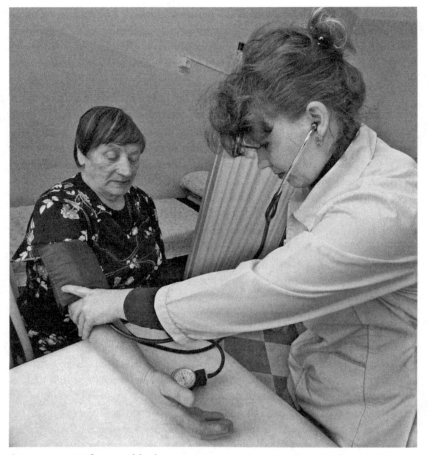

A nurse cares for an elderly patient at a retirement home. *(RIA Novosti/ TopFoto, The Image Works)*

tation required by HMOs, the federal government, and insurance providers.

Gerontological nurse practitioners are registered nurses who have advanced training and education. This training enables them to carry out many of the responsibilities traditionally handled by physicians. Gerontological nurse practitioners are often based in nursing homes and work with older adults.

Gerontological clinical nurse specialists conduct health assessments and evaluations of elderly patients based on their history, laboratory tests, and their own personal examinations. Following such assessments they arrive at a diagnosis of the patient's problem and deliver care and develop quality-control methods to help correct the patient's medical problem.

Advancement into administration positions such as nursing home administrator or director of nursing is common for persons involved in a geriatric nursing career.

REQUIREMENTS

High School

If you are interested in a geriatric nursing career, be prepared to continue your education after high school. You should take a general college preparatory curriculum, which will include studies in history, social sciences, science, math, English, and computer science. Science and math classes, such as biology, chemistry, physics, algebra, and geometry, will be particularly important to take. Taking four years of English classes is also recommended because these classes will enhance your ability to research, write, and speak effectively. In addition, you should consider taking a foreign language, which will further broaden your communication skills.

Postsecondary Training

To work as a geriatric nurse, you must first become a registered nurse (R.N.). There are three basic kinds of training programs that you can choose from to become an R.N.: associate's degree programs, diploma programs, and bachelor's degree programs. The associate in arts in nursing is awarded after completion of a two-year program, which is usually offered by junior or community colleges. You receive hospital training at cooperating hospitals in the general vicinity of the community college. The diploma program, which usually lasts three years, is conducted by hospitals and independent schools.

Perhaps the best route, however, is the bachelor's degree program. One reason is that you will have more time to study a variety of topics in a four-year bachelor's program. As the need for geriatric nurses has grown, more and more bachelor's programs have begun to incorporate classes on gerontological nursing or care of older adults into their core curriculums. This degree will also provide the most career mobility, because a bachelor's degree is required for most supervisory or administrative positions, for jobs in public health agencies, and for admission to graduate nursing programs. The bachelor's of science (B.S.) in nursing is offered by colleges and universities and takes four (in some cases, five) years to complete. Besides taking courses to fulfill your college's general requirements, typical courses you may encounter in a B.S. nursing program include health assessment, pharmacology, nursing care of adults, health policy and issues, gerontological nursing, and management strategies. Once you have completed any one of these three programs, you must take and pass a licensing examination that is required in all states to become an R.N.

To become a gerontological nurse, you'll need to gain experience working in gerontology, and, if you fulfill other requirements, you can become certified as a gerontological nurse by the American Nurses Credentialing Center (ANCC). If you would like to advance into a specialty position, a position with more responsibilities, or a position teaching at a college or university, you will need to pursue additional education. With a master's degree, you can work as a gerontological nurse practitioner or a clinical specialist in gerontological nursing. Nurses in these advanced positions are able to diagnose and treat common illnesses. In addition, they can have prescriptive authority; that is, they can write prescriptions for their patients. Nurses wanting to pursue research need to complete a doctorate degree. The National League for Nursing Accrediting Commission is responsible for accrediting all types of nursing programs offering a certificate, diploma, undergraduate, or graduate degree. The Commission on Collegiate Nursing Education, part of the American Association of Colleges of Nursing, also accredits nursing programs. Both groups provide information on these approved programs.

Certification or Licensing

Certification is available from the ANCC and is highly recommended. Candidates with current R.N. licenses and a certain amount of experience in the area of practice (gerontology) are eligible to take the specialty and informatics exam. Nurse practitioners and clinical nursing specialists who fulfill certain eligibility requirements and pass an exam can become board certified as advanced practice registered nurses.

All nurses must be licensed to work in the state in which they are employed. They must graduate from an accredited nursing program and pass a national licensing examination to obtain this license. Nurses who wish to specialize in hospice or home health care may choose to attend graduate school.

Other Requirements

Geriatric nurses should enjoy working with and being around older people. They must have a general interest in aging and understand the problems related to growing older. Geriatric nurses must have the ability to get along with the patient's family members and must be able to work well with other professionals such as hospice nurses, chaplains, and social workers. Being able to work as part of a team is essential since many people may become involved in the health care and health needs of the elderly person. Communication skills are also essential. The nurse must be able to communicate with the family and the patient and explain medical terminology and procedures to them so they understand what is being done and why.

EXPLORING

You can explore your interest in nursing and in working with older people in a number of ways. Read books and visit Web sites that deal with the nursing profession. Ask your high school counselor to help you arrange for an information interview with a local nurse. Your school nurse is also someone to consult about the profession and the education required for it. Many hospitals have volunteer programs that provide the opportunity to work during the summer or on a part-time basis, escorting patients to tests, delivering flowers to patients' rooms, and doing other helpful tasks. Volunteering at a hospital will give you a lot of insight as to how hospitals work and how well you like this environment.

To explore how much you enjoy working with older people, volunteer at a senior center, where you may be able to sit in on a card game or teach a crafts project. Volunteer positions as well as part-time or summer jobs also may be available at a nursing home in your area. Use any opportunity you can to visit with older people in your community. You will learn a lot from being around them, and they may be just as eager to learn something from you.

EMPLOYERS

Geriatric nurses work in a variety of settings, depending on their education and personal goals. Many geriatric nurses work in nursing homes, hospitals, retirement communities, or clinics. They may also work in hospice and home care or community nursing programs; others work in private offices for gerontologists or at government agencies. Nurses who teach or do research are most often in academic settings, usually in buildings that are well lighted, comfortable, and busy.

STARTING OUT

Once you have become a registered nurse, you can apply directly to hospitals, nursing homes, government agencies, and other organizations that hire nurses and offer opportunities to work with older patients. In addition, your school's career services office should have information on job openings. Nurses' associations and their Web sites, professional journals, and newspapers also frequently advertise open positions.

ADVANCEMENT

Advancement in this field often comes with further education. Those with bachelor's degrees can obtain graduate degrees and work as gerontological nurse practitioners or clinical specialists in gerontological nursing. These nurses have greater responsibilities and command higher salaries. Other specialties, such as medications nurse and charge nurse, also require advanced education. Nurses who obtain additional education in administration and management may move into administration positions at nursing departments, hospitals, or nursing homes.

EARNINGS

According to the U.S. Department of Labor, registered nurses earned a median annual salary of $63,750 in 2009. The lowest paid 10 percent earned less than $43,970, while the middle 50 percent earned between $52,520 and $77,970. The top paid 10 percent made more than $93,700 a year. Registered nurses employed in home health care settings earned mean annual salaries of $63,300, and those who worked at nursing care facilities earned $59,320. Registered nurses who worked in hospice settings earned hourly salaries that ranged from $24.23 to $28.50 in 2008–09, according to the Hospital and Healthcare Compensation Service and the Hospice Association of America. Licensed practical nurses earned between $16.83 and $20.76. Nurse practitioners and clinical nurse specialists typically earn higher salaries.

Salary is determined by many factors, including nursing specialty, education, and place of employment, shift worked, geographical location, and work experience. Flexible schedules and part-time employment opportunities are available for most nurses. Employers usually provide health and life insurance, and some offer educational reimbursements and year-end bonuses to their full-time staff.

WORK ENVIRONMENT

Geriatric nurses can expect to work in a variety of settings depending on their nursing responsibilities. Many geriatric nurses work in nursing homes, hospitals, retirement communities, or in clinics. They may also work with hospice and community nursing programs, or as office nurses for gerontologists.

Although most health care environments will be clean and well lighted, there may be some nursing situations where the surroundings may be less than desirable. Some nurses are on call 24 hours a day and may be required to travel to homes in all neighborhoods of a city or in remote rural areas day and night. Safety may be an issue at times.

All nursing careers have some health and disease risks; however, adherence to health and safety guidelines greatly minimizes the chance of contracting infectious diseases such as hepatitis and AIDS. Medical knowledge and good safety measures are also needed to limit the nurse's exposure to toxic chemicals, radiation, and other hazards.

OUTLOOK

Nursing specialties will be in great demand in the future. The U.S. Department of Labor predicts that the number of new jobs for registered nurses will be among the largest for any occupation. Most of these jobs will result from current nurses reaching retirement age, in addition to the many technological advances in medicine that will create a need for more people to administer patient care.

Job opportunities for individuals who enter geriatric nursing are predicted to grow at a rate that is much faster than the average for all careers. The Administration on Aging estimates that the number of individuals aged 65 or older will double by 2030. As the older population increases, their need for medical care will also increase. In addition, a 2001 report by the Nursing Institute at the University of Illinois predicts that the ratio of caregivers to the elderly population will decrease by 40 percent between 2010 and 2030. As a result, employment prospects for qualified geriatric nurses are nearly limitless.

FOR MORE INFORMATION

For information on education and scholarships, as well as an overview of expected competencies for geriatric nurses, visit the association's Web site.

American Association of Colleges of Nursing
One Dupont Circle, NW, Suite 530
Washington, DC 20036-1135
Tel: 202-463-6930
http://www.aacn.nche.edu

For information about critical care nursing, contact
American Association of Critical-Care Nurses
101 Columbia
Aliso Viejo, CA 92656-4109

E-mail: info@aacn.org
http://www.aacn.org

*To read profiles of geriatric care professionals, visit the society's
Web site.*
American Geriatrics Society
350 Fifth Avenue, Suite 801
New York, NY 10118-0801
Tel: 212-308-1414
E-mail: info@americangeriatrics.org
http://www.americangeriatrics.org

*For information about advanced practice gerontological nursing,
contact*
Gerontological Advanced Practice Nurses Association
East Holly Avenue, Box 56
Pitman, NJ 08071-0056
Tel: 866-355-1392
https://www.gapna.org

For general information about hospice care, contact
National Association for Home Care and Hospice
228 Seventh Street, SE
Washington, DC 20003-4306
Tel: 202-547-7424
http://www.nahc.org

For information about a career as a clinical nurse specialist, contact
National Association of Clinical Nurse Specialists
100 North 20th Street, 4th Floor
Philadelphia, PA 19103-1443
Tel: 215-320-3881
http://www.nacns.org

For information about geriatric nursing, contact
National Gerontological Nursing Association
7794 Grow Drive
Pensacola, FL 32514-7072
Tel: 800-723-0560
E-mail: info@ngna.org
http://www.ngna.org

For industry statistics, contact
National Hospice and Palliative Care Organization
1731 King Street, Suite 100
Alexandria, VA 22314-2720
Tel: 703-837-1500
E-mail: nhpco_info@nhpco.org
http://www.nhpco.org

For career information, contact
Visiting Nurse Associations of America
900 19th Street, NW, Suite 200
Washington, DC 20006-2122
Tel: 202-384-1420
E-mail: vnaa@vnaa.org
http://vnaa.org

Geriatric Psychiatrists

QUICK FACTS

School Subjects
English
Psychology
Biology

Personal Skills
Helping/teaching
Technical/scientific

Work Environment
Primarily indoors
One location with some
travel

Minimum Education Level
Medical degree

Salary Range
$47,458 to $160,230 to
$248,198

Certification or Licensing
Required for certain positions (certification)
Required by all states (licensing)

Outlook
Much faster than the average

DOT
070

GOE
14.02.01

NOC
3111

O*NET-SOC
29.1066.00

OVERVIEW

Geriatric psychiatrists are physicians who attend to elderly patients' mental, emotional, and behavioral symptoms. They treat older patients who may suffer from dementia or depression or have other mental illnesses, and they employ different methods to help them function better in their daily lives. For example, geriatric psychiatrists may prescribe medicine, including tranquilizers, antipsychotics, and antidepressants, to help their patients feel better. The medication may also be combined with another therapeutic approach, such as talk therapy. In addition, geriatric psychiatrists may assist nursing home staff and other caregivers in developing individualized treatment programs and approaches designed to bring improvement to patients.

HISTORY

Although mental illness has been observed and documented for hundreds of years, the major advances in psychiatric treatment came in the latter part of the 19th century. Emil Kraepelin, a German psychiatrist, made an important contribution when he developed a classification system for mental illnesses that is still used for diagnosis. Sigmund Freud, the famous Viennese psychiatrist, developed techniques for analyzing human behavior that have strongly influenced the practice of modern psychiatry.

In the 20th century, the practice of psychiatry underwent another major advancement with the development of medications that could be used in treating psychiatric problems, such as depression and

Facts About Alzheimer's Disease

Alzheimer's disease causes a person's brain cells to deteriorate and die over the course of several years. The disease is marked by memory loss, dementia, and, eventually, death from loss of brain function. The following are some Alzheimer's statistics from the Alzheimer's Association:

- Approximately 5.3 million Americans have Alzheimer's disease. It is the seventh leading cause of death in the United States.

- By 2050, approximately 11 to 16 million Americans will be diagnosed with Alzheimer's disease unless a cure or prevention is found.

- Thirteen percent of people over the age of 65 have Alzheimer's disease. Nearly 50 percent of those over age 85 have the disease.

- A small percentage of people get the disease while they are in their 30s or 40s.

- After the onset of symptoms, people with Alzheimer's disease live an average of eight years.

- Seven out of 10 people with Alzheimer's disease live at home and receive most of their care from family or friends. Neither Medicare nor most private health insurance covers the expense of long-term care that most patients need.

- Nearly half of all nursing home residents suffer from Alzheimer's disease or a related disorder.

anxiety. Since then, great strides have been made in this area, and medication is very often a component of psychiatric treatment.

The past several decades have seen new challenges emerge in the field, especially in regard to the elderly and their mental health. Medical, industrial, and technological breakthroughs have brought a substantial increase in Americans' life spans. This increase means we have a growing elderly population. The Administration on Aging predicts that the number of Americans age 65 and older will more than double in the first three decades of the 21st century, increasing from 35 million in 2000 to approximately 71.5 million in 2030.

Some elderly people in nursing homes and long-term care facilities have a mental illness. Currently, though, most are not getting proper psychiatric treatment; in fact, the vast majority are not receiving psychiatric attention at all. Nursing homes were designed to treat people's physical, not mental, problems, and until fairly recently the mental health issues of elderly people were not even recognized by most people, even physicians. Professional recognition for the field of geriatric psychiatry was obtained in 1991 when it was formally recognized as a subspecialty of psychiatry and in 1998 when the American Psychological Association voted to recognize that clinical practice with the elderly requires special training, expertise, and skill.

The growing number of senior citizens in the United States and the proliferation and recognition of Alzheimer's disease, dementia, depression, and other mental diseases and disorders of the elderly point to the need for geriatric psychiatrists.

THE JOB

Geriatric psychiatrists treat elderly patients who suffer from mental and emotional illnesses that make it hard for them to cope with everyday living or to behave in socially acceptable ways. The most common problems treated are dementia and depression, although the elderly can have the same range of disorders as the rest of the population. Often, though, these disorders are not properly diagnosed. According to an article in *Psychiatric News,* experts estimated that one in five seniors has clinically significant anxiety and one in 12 is dependent on alcohol. In addition, these estimates may actually be low since mental illnesses in the elderly are often misdiagnosed or missed altogether.

Geriatric psychiatrists evaluate their patients using a variety of methods, depending on the patient's ability to articulate his or her thoughts and feelings and on the psychiatrist's preferred techniques and practice methods. Geriatric psychiatrists sometimes face special challenges in determining what might be causing erratic or problematic behavior in patients who are unable to express themselves well; sometimes the source of an inappropriate behavior is something relatively simple, such as a minor health problem. By correctly diagnosing problems, the psychiatrist can not only save the patient distress and discomfort but also avert inappropriate treatments that may be costly and to the patient's detriment.

In other cases, geriatric psychiatrists have to distinguish between the naturally occurring emotional complexities of aging and true illness. Sadness and grief are unquestionably a part of old age. As people reach the last stages of life, they experience many losses, from deterioration of their health and body to deaths of spouses, family members, and friends. The line between this natural sadness and genuine clinical depression can be a thin one. A geriatric psychiatrist must recognize symptoms that point to a genuine depression and treat it accordingly. Just as important, however, the psychiatrist must avoid "medicating away" some of the natural, inescapable feelings that accompany age. Some feelings of sadness may be normal as people realize they have little time left. Part of the geriatric psychiatrist's complex work is to determine what's normal, what's not, and the best course of action in either case.

Because geriatric psychiatrists are medical doctors, they typically begin their patient evaluations with a range of medical tests, including physical and neurological evaluations, laboratory tests, and X-rays. These tests will often reveal physical causes for behavioral problems and can result in the psychiatrist referring the patient to a specialist for the needed physical care.

Some psychiatrists rely largely on certain therapeutic techniques in their practices, such as talk therapy or behavior therapy. Naturally, though, these methods are only effective in those willing to try them and grow from the experience. Some people with impairments, such as patients in the late stages of Alzheimer's disease, may not have the ability to process their emotions or communicate clearly. These people may benefit from different therapies. Pharmacotherapy, which is the use of psychotherapeutic medications, such as antidepressants, mood-stabilizing drugs, and tranquilizers, is often used to help elderly patients. Because of this, geriatric psychiatrists must be knowledgeable about potential drug interaction problems, as elderly patients often take a variety of medications for physical problems, such as high cholesterol, arthritis, or diabetes.

No matter what therapy techniques psychiatrists prefer, however, they must individualize treatment programs to meet each patient's needs. Many older people are lonely and simply having someone to talk to on a regular basis can make an extraordinary difference in their attitude and outlook. For other patients, however, talk therapy alone isn't enough to help them feel better, and they benefit from taking medication. The psychiatrist may also use other techniques, such as art therapy (which involves participating in music, dance, or media art), occupational therapy (in which patients learn or relearn skills for caring for themselves), or group therapy (during which a number of patients discuss their personal problems), to help the patient.

An unavoidable component of geriatric psychiatrists' job is paperwork. They must do a large amount of documentation, both in keeping patient records up to date and in dealing with Medicare, Medicaid, HMOs, and other insurance companies. More and more psychiatrists, like other health care professionals, are reporting that getting through the increasing amount of red tape and meeting requirements for documentation are encroaching on the time they otherwise would have used to see patients.

Although many geriatric psychiatrists are in private practice, it is likely to become more common for nursing homes and other facilities to employ geriatric psychiatrists full time to better meet the needs of their residents. In this environment, the psychiatrist works as a member of a multidisciplinary team, including other nursing home staff. The team shares information, develops appropriate therapeutic approaches, and monitors the treatment for each patient. Because the number of elderly people in our country is large and growing rapidly, geriatric psychiatrists should have many opportunities. Nursing homes and other care facilities that have geriatric psychiatrists on staff will be seen by seniors and their families as institutions that offer quality care.

REQUIREMENTS

High School

If you think medical school is in your future, you should focus on college preparatory classes in high school. Take plenty of science and math courses, including biology, chemistry, physics, algebra, and calculus. To prepare for your later psychology studies, take sociology, psychology, and history classes. English courses that teach you to research, write, and speak well are also important, as you will need to express yourself clearly not only to patients but also to the other professionals you'll be working with.

Postsecondary Training

Since you will need to attend medical school to become a geriatric psychiatrist, you should plan your college curriculum to meet medical school admission requirements. You will benefit from consulting the Association of American Medical Colleges' annual publication *Medical School Admission Requirements* (which is also available online at http://www.aamc.org/students/applying/msar.htm). It has information on schools' entrance requirements, as well as information on other topics such as schools' curricula and financial aid. Typical majors for those planning on attending medical school include biology, chemistry, and biochemistry. You should also continue to take psychology and English classes. Some universities now offer undergraduate courses in gerontology that cover topics such as the sociology of aging and public policy issues affecting the elderly. Scores from the Medical College Admission Test (http://www.aamc.org/students/mcat/start.htm) are required for admission by most medical schools. Students usually take this test during their junior year of college.

In medical school, you will need to complete a four-year program of medical studies and supervised clinical work to earn your M.D. degree. Most instruction in the first two years is given through classroom lectures, laboratories, seminars, and the reading of textbook material. You will also learn to take medical histories, examine patients, and recognize symptoms.

During the last two years of medical school, you will become actively involved in the treatment process, spending a large proportion of your time in the hospital as part of a medical team headed by a teaching physician. You will be closely supervised as you learn techniques such as how to take a patient's medical history, how to make a physical examination, how to work in the laboratory, how to make a diagnosis, and how to keep all the necessary records. In addition to this hospital work, you will continue to take course work.

Psychiatrists can also attend an osteopathic medical program leading to the Doctor of Osteopathic Medicine (D.O.).

Once you have completed four years of medical school, you will need to complete a residency. First-year residents work in several specialties, such as pediatrics or internal medicine. After that, residents wanting to become psychiatrists complete three years of work at a psychiatric hospital or a general hospital's psychiatric ward. In addition, residents may complete a geriatric psychiatry fellowship, a program typically lasting one year and providing specialized geriatric training. Completing such a fellowship is highly recommended.

Certification or Licensing

The American Board of Psychiatry and Neurology (ABPN) is the certifying board for all psychiatrists, regardless of their specialty. To become an ABPN-certified psychiatrist, you will need to pass a written and an oral test. An ABPN-certified psychiatrist may treat geriatric patients. Those in the field, however, recommend that you complete a geriatric psychiatry fellowship program, which qualifies you to apply for the subspecialty certification of geriatric psychiatrist. To obtain this subspecialty certification, also available through ABPN, you must pass a written exam covering topics such as psychological and social aspects of aging and diagnostic methods. This certification is highly recommended because it will enhance your professional standing as well as demonstrate to your patients and their families your extensive training in this field.

After receiving their M.D. or D.O. degree, all doctors must pass a licensing test in order to practice medicine in the state in which they will work. Depending on the requirements of your state, you may need to pass the National Board of Medical Examiners test or an individual state licensing test. Because these requirements vary, you will need to check with your state's licensing board for specific information.

Other Requirements

Geriatric psychiatrists need to be compassionate, patient, flexible, and intelligent. To be effective in their work, they must understand a vast array of medical, technical, and psychological information. They need analyzing and diagnosing skills, excellent listening skills, and administrative skills. Decision-making ability, time-management skills, and writing skills are also important in this career. Like any doctor, they must be committed to lifelong learning in order to keep up with advancements in the field, such as new medications.

Perhaps most important, though, geriatric psychiatrists must enjoy working with older people, listening to them and helping them with their unique set of problems. A successful geriatric psychiatrist must have a firm belief that, with the right treatment, mentally ill seniors can get relief from their pain and lead improved and fulfilling lives.

EXPLORING

You should take advantage of any available opportunities to learn more about the psychiatric field and about working with the elderly. Use your local library or search the Internet for resources on the field. You can learn about psychotherapy in general by reading books such as *Inside Therapy: Illuminating Writings about Therapists, Patients, and Psychotherapy,* edited by Ilana Rabinowitz (New York: St. Martin's Griffin, 2000) and *Essential Psychotherapies: Theory and Practice,* 2nd edition, edited by Alan Gurman and Stanley Messer (New York: The Guilford Press, 2005). You can also take a look at articles from the *American Journal of Geriatric Psychiatry,* which is the official publication for the American Association for Geriatric Psychiatry. Articles from the journal are available online at http://journals.lww.com/ajgponline. You can also ask your high school counselor for help in setting up an information interview with a local psychiatrist or other physician. Even if you are only able to talk to a family doctor, you can still ask him or her what medical school was like, what college courses were particularly helpful to take, and other general questions about the profession.

It is very important that you get experience working with the elderly. Hands-on experience will allow you to find out how much you like working with this group of people, and it will make you a more desirable candidate when you apply to colleges and medical schools. Begin in high school by getting a summer or part-time job at a hospital, clinic, senior day program, or nursing home. High school students can seek jobs as certified nursing assistants, which would provide hands-on experience taking care of geriatric patients. If you are unable to find paid work, become a volunteer.

EMPLOYERS

Approximately half of all practicing psychiatrists work in private practice; many others combine private practice with work in a health care institution. These institutions include private hospitals, state mental hospitals, medical schools, community health centers, and government health agencies. Psychiatrists also work for health maintenance organizations and in nursing homes. They are employed throughout the country.

While it is still most common for geriatric psychiatrists to work either alone or as part of a group in private practice, there will likely be a growing trend for skilled nursing facilities to employ full-time psychiatrists. This serves to improve care to residents because the psychiatrist is able to form ongoing relationships with the patients as well as ongoing relationships with the staff. In addition, the psychiatrist can work closely with the staff on treatment plans and give advice or instruction on how to deal with the various challenges facing the patients.

STARTING OUT

Professional journals and organizations (such as the American Psychiatric Association and the American Association for Geriatric Psychiatry) can provide good job leads for beginning geriatric psychiatrists. Many doctors are offered permanent positions with the same institution where they completed their residency. Those new psychiatrists who choose to specialize in geriatrics may have an advantage because the rapidly increasing numbers of elderly people means a growing client base. In nursing homes and in general, this population is underserved and in particular need of access to psychiatric services.

ADVANCEMENT

In geriatric psychiatry as well as other physician specialties, advancement usually comes in the form of an increased clientele and increased earnings that result from the psychiatrist's good reputation, skills, and up-to-date knowledge. Those who work in hospitals, clinics, and mental health centers may choose to advance by becoming administrators. Other geriatric psychiatrists may be drawn to research and academia, where they may advance to become department heads.

EARNINGS

Like other physicians, psychiatrists' average income is among the highest of all professionals. Psychiatrists' earnings are determined by their experience, number of patients, location, and type of practice.

First-year medical interns earned $47,458 in 2009, according to the Association of American Medical Colleges. Psychiatrists earned median annual salaries of $160,230 in 2009, according to the U.S. Department of Labor. Psychiatrists working in nursing care facilities earned mean annual salaries of $199,910 in 2009. Salaries for psychiatrists ranged from $173,800 to $248,198, according to *Modern Healthcare*'s 2008 Physician Compensation Survey.

Psychiatrists who are employed by health care institution receive fringe benefits such as health insurance and paid vacation and sick days. Those who are self-employed must provide their own benefits.

WORK ENVIRONMENT

Geriatric psychiatrists in private practice set their own schedules and usually work regular hours. While other kinds of psychiatrists are likely to work some evenings or weekends to accommodate patients who work, geriatric psychiatrists' patients typically have fairly open daytime schedules. Some geriatric psychiatrists work as few as 35 to 40 hours a week; others might work as many as 70. This depends on the type of practice, the size of the clientele, and the personal goals and desires of the psychiatrist. Geriatric psychiatrists, like other kinds of psychiatrists, may spend a certain amount of time on call. This means they need to be accessible to their patients and available to handle or advise on any crisis that might arise.

Geriatric psychiatrists in private practice typically work in comfortable office settings. Other settings may vary; consulting work in nursing homes might be somewhat less comfortable, both because the environment can be disturbing or depressing at times and because the psychiatrist may not have a designated work area. Because many geriatric psychiatrists work in a consultant capacity to various nursing or day facilities, they are more likely than other psychiatrists and physicians to commute with some frequency and work in multiple locations.

OUTLOOK

Job opportunities for physicians in general are expected to grow much faster than the average for all careers through 2018, according to the U.S. Department of Labor. Opportunities for geriatric psychiatrists both in private practice and in salaried positions are excellent. The demand for psychiatrists serving seniors is high, and the demand is growing each year as this population increases.

As the importance of mental health care for our elderly is increasingly recognized and accepted, it should become easier for seniors and their families to have access to and support in securing treatment. One concern that may limit the number of elderly seeking mental health care is financial. Medicare payments for psychiatric treatments are very limited, and good care is expensive. Government health care reforms, however, may make mental health care available to more people.

In addition to the need for geriatric psychiatrists to work in clinical practice (seeing patients), there is a strong need for geriatric psychiatrists to work in research and academia. Overall, employment in this field should grow at a strong rate.

FOR MORE INFORMATION

For resources aimed at older people, their families, and their caregivers, visit the administration's Web site.
Administration on Aging
Washington, DC 20201-0001
Tel: 202-619-0724
E-mail: aoainfo@aoa.hhs.gov
http://www.aoa.gov

For information about Alzheimer's disease, caregiving, and local chapters of the association, contact
Alzheimer's Association
225 North Michigan Avenue, Floor 17
Chicago, IL 60601-7633
Tel: 800-272-3900
E-mail: info@alz.org
http://www.alz.org

For information on geriatric psychiatry, contact
American Association for Geriatric Psychiatry
7910 Woodmont Avenue
Bethesda, MD 20814-3004
Tel: 301-654-7850
E-mail: main@aagponline.org
http://www.aagpgpa.org

For information on board certification, contact
American Board of Psychiatry and Neurology
2150 East Lake Cook Road, Suite 900
Buffalo Grove, IL 60089-1875
Tel: 847-229-6500
http://www.abpn.com

For information on choosing a medical specialty, as well as a description of psychiatry, contact
American Medical Association
515 North State Street
Chicago, IL 60654-4854
Tel: 800-621-8335
http://www.ama-assn.org

For information on osteopathic medicine, visit the AOA Web site.
American Osteopathic Association (AOA)
142 East Ontario Street
Chicago, IL 60611-2874
Tel: 800-621-1773
http://www.osteopathic.org

For comprehensive information on careers in psychiatry, contact
American Psychiatric Association
1000 Wilson Boulevard, Suite 1825
Arlington, VA 22209-3901
Tel: 888-357-7924
E-mail: apa@psych.org
http://www.psych.org

To learn more about careers in medicine and how to apply to medical schools, visit the association's Web site.
Association of American Medical Colleges
2450 N Street, NW
Washington, DC 20037-1126
Tel: 202-828-0400
http://www.aamc.org

For information on mental health, and to read the newsletter The Bell, *which contains current information about the field, visit the association's Web site.*
Mental Health America
2000 North Beauregard Street, 6th Floor
Alexandria, VA 22311-1748

Tel: 703-684-7722
http://www.nmha.org

For information on mental health issues, contact
National Institute of Mental Health
Science Writing, Press, and Dissemination Branch
6001 Executive Boulevard, Room 8184, MSC 9663
Bethesda, MD 20892-9663
Tel: 866-615-6464
E-mail: nimhinfo@nih.gov
http://www.nimh.nih.gov

For information about improving the health and well-being of older
Americans through research, contact
National Institute on Aging
Building 31, Room 5C27
31 Center Drive, MSC 2292
Bethesda, MD 20892-0001
Tel: 301-496-1752
http://www.nia.nih.gov

Geriatric Social Workers

QUICK FACTS

School Subjects
Psychology
Sociology

Personal Skills
Helping/teaching
Leadership/management

Work Environment
Primarily indoors
Primarily multiple locations

Minimum Education Level
Bachelor's degree

Salary Range
$24,940 to $46,300 to
$71,190+

Certification or Licensing
Recommended (certification)
Required by all states
(licensing)

Outlook
Much faster than the average

DOT
195

GOE
12.02.02

NOC
4152

O*NET-SOC
21-1021.00, 21-1022.00,
21-1023.00, 21-1029.00

OVERVIEW

Geriatric social workers, also known as *gerontology social workers,* help elderly people adjust to the challenges of growing older. They develop programs and direct agencies that offer counseling, advocacy, and special services. They evaluate the needs of clients and help them arrange for such things as meal service, housing, transportation, and legal and medical assistance. Geriatric social workers also develop recreation and educational programs for the elderly.

Approximately one-third of all social workers work with older people. They work in hospitals, nursing homes, and retirement communities; they have offices in human service agencies and senior centers. Geriatric social workers must have a genuine interest in the well-being of older people and must be sensitive to their concerns and problems.

HISTORY

Social workers were often the villains of old movies. They were often portrayed as either stiff, unemotional women carrying briefcases and wearing long dark skirts, or as thin, bald men with beady eyes behind thick glasses. With little emotion, they dragged children off to orphanages, committed sane people to insane asylums, and threatened the poor and elderly. The goal of the social worker seemed to be to uphold social norms by breaking up unconventional families. This may reflect a moral superiority that tainted social work up until the early 20th century. Today, the social services industry is responsible for empowering individuals (such as the poor, elderly, and ill) and helping them to face personal problems and address large social issues.

Theories and methodologies of social work have changed over the years, but the basis of the profession has remained the same: helping people address hardships such as poverty, illness, drug addictions, and aging. As society changes, so do its problems, calling for redefinition of the social work profession. The U.S. population is getting older. Changing demographics have created a need for experienced professionals in geriatrics. Geriatric social workers help older individuals and their families to cope with the difficulties encountered in aging, such as maintaining mental and physical health and overcoming feelings of depression or fears of dying.

THE JOB

A woman in her late 70s has just lost her husband and now must live alone for the first time in many years. She has decided to move to another town to live closer to her children and will need help making the transition. She needs a smaller, more manageable home; she needs help with meals and shopping; she would like to make friends in the community. A number of services are available to her, but she may not find out about them without the aid of a geriatric social worker.

As with any social worker, the geriatric social worker is devoted to helping people and communities solve problems. Social workers are dedicated to empowering people and helping people to preserve their dignity and feeling of worth. This kind of assistance and advocacy is especially important among older people. Because old age can sometimes put a person in poor physical and mental health as well as cause financial difficulties, older people often need help and protection. They may need help with preparing meals, finding transportation, and doing housework, or they may need assistance moving into a retirement community or nursing home. But the elderly population of any community is diverse; some older people stay in perfectly good health, and they rely on social services for recreation, meeting people, educational programs, and grief and loss counseling.

People are living longer these days, and the elderly population is growing. At the beginning of the 20th century, only one-half of newborns would live past the age of 50; people born at the beginning of the 21st century can, on average, expect to live well past the age of 75. This is why geriatric social work will continue to offer many job opportunities.

The social work profession is divided into two areas: direct practice and indirect practice. Direct practice is also known as clinical practice. As the name suggests, direct practice involves working directly with the client by offering counseling, advocacy, information and referral, and education. Indirect practice (a practice consisting mostly of social workers who hold Ph.D.'s) concerns the structures through which the direct practice is offered. Indirect practice involves program development and evaluation, administration, and policy analysis. Geriatric social workers may work directly with the elderly population through counseling, advising, and conducting group sessions. They also help clients find services for health, housing, finances, and transportation. Those geriatric social workers involved in indirect practice develop and oversee the agencies and departments that provide these social services.

Geriatric social workers work for service agencies, hospitals, nursing homes, senior centers, and other community organizations. Some also work independently. Their help is needed in every town and city across the country; some social workers in areas with smaller populations may serve a number of small towns within a region. No matter where a geriatric social worker serves, the nature of the work is usually the same. Geriatric social workers meet with older people individually to determine their needs. Home meal delivery programs, transportation services, and recreational programs are some of the basic services offered by community organizations. Some organizations also offer home health care. With nurses and aides assigned to visit the elderly in their homes and to help them with their housework and medical needs, elderly clients can continue to live on their own.

Geriatric social workers evaluate clients by interviewing them and determining their needs; social workers then enroll clients for these services. They make phone calls and provide the service agencies with client information.

The client may need even more assistance. Adult day care services are available in some cities, as are adult foster care services that match older people with families. A social worker may also need to help a client arrange to move into a nursing home and counsel the client about the transition. These counseling services are also extended to members of the client's family, advising them in how to deal with a parent's or grandparent's aging or illness.

In some cases, an elderly person is neglected or taken advantage of. A geriatric social worker can look into these cases and serve as an advocate, stepping in to advise the client of his or her legal rights. In addition to legal services, a geriatric social worker will help a client locate any needed financial services. Social workers help clients make arrangements for the payment of services through Medicare and other financial aid.

Because of efforts by the government to improve the quality of nursing home care, social workers are becoming more active within these facilities. These geriatric social workers work closely with the elderly and their families in arranging the move into the nursing home. They also counsel families upon the death of an elderly relative and help with funeral arrangements. Geriatric social workers also protect and promote the rights of the residents, and they may train nursing care staff members on patient rights.

The geriatric social worker is part of the larger field of aging. This field, which works to provide help for older people while researching the process of aging, is composed of hospitals, health care corporations, government agencies, churches, colleges, and other organizations and institutions. Various professions, such as law, psychology, health care, education, and marketing, include specialties in aging, or gerontology.

REQUIREMENTS

High School

Since you will need at least a bachelor's degree to advance in this field, prepare by taking a college preparatory curriculum in high school. This should include math, science, and computer science classes. Other courses that will help you in this field include civics or government courses, in which you can learn about the enactment of laws, such as the Older Americans Act. Psychology and sociology courses will help you gain an understanding of human behavior and the process of aging as well as teach you methods for studying groups of people, such as the elderly. Take English classes to develop your writing, speaking, and researching skills—skills that you will need throughout your career.

Postsecondary Training

A minimum of a bachelor's degree in social work, psychology, sociology, or a related field is required for employment as a geriatric social worker, although many employers now require applicants to have a master's degree. The Council on Social Work Education, which accredits bachelor's and master's programs in social work, has approved 468 programs granting the bachelor's degree in social work (B.S.W.) and 196 programs granting the master's degree (M.S.W.). The council offers a listing of member programs at its Web site, http://www.cswe.org. The Group for the Advancement of Doctoral Education in Social Work (http://www.gadephd.org) provides contact information for more than 70 programs that offer the doctor of social work (D.S.W.) degree or the Ph.D. in social work. Accredited B.S.W. programs include courses in human behavior and the social environment, social welfare policy and services, social work practice, research, and field practicum. Most programs require two years of liberal arts study, followed by two years of study in the social work major. Students must also complete a field practicum of at least 400 hours.

Although no clear lines of classification are drawn in the social work profession, most supervisory and administrative positions require at least a master's degree in social work. Master's programs are organized according to fields of practice (such as mental health care), problem areas (substance abuse), population groups (the elderly), and practice roles (practice with individuals, families, or communities). They are usually two-year programs, requiring at least 900 hours of field practice.

Doctoral degrees are usually necessary for research and teaching. Many social workers with doctorates work in community organizations.

Certification or Licensing

The National Association of Social Workers (NASW) offers certification in several areas. All social workers who meet requirements, which include education, experience, and passing an exam, may receive the designation academy of certified social workers. In addition, the NASW offers specialty certifications, and certification as a qualified clinical social worker and as a diplomate in clinical social work to those who meet specific education, practice, and other requirements. Although certification is voluntary, it is highly recommended for anyone wanting to advance in the field. Certification demonstrates that you have gained the knowledge and experience necessary to meet national standards.

The practice of social work is regulated in all states and the District of Columbia. To receive the necessary licensing, a social worker typically has to gain a certain amount of experience and pass an exam. Because requirements vary by state, you will need to check with the regulatory board in your state for specific information. Licensing information is also available from the Association of Social Work Boards.

Other Requirements

To be a successful geriatric social worker, you must care about the needs and problems of older people. Many of these people will be relying on you to help them through crucial and difficult times; you must be completely dedicated to your clients and devoted to helping them maintain their dignity and sense of self-worth.

Most geriatric social workers are involved directly with the people they serve, and they are expected to carefully examine a client's living habits and family relations. A geriatric social worker has to be prepared to confront depressing situations occasionally. In most cases, though, a good geriatric social worker will take pleasure from helping a client through a rough time and will take pride in seeing the client improve his or her life. It is also important for a geriatric social worker to be good-natured and friendly; clients resistant to change may refuse to cooperate with someone they find unpleasant. A geriatric social worker must be very sensitive to the problems of the elderly but must also remain supportive and encouraging.

EXPLORING

Ask a counselor or teacher to arrange an information interview with a geriatric social worker. Read books and magazines about geriatric care. Volunteering is one of the best ways to explore your interest in geriatric social work. Check with nursing homes, senior care centers, or organizations such as Meals on Wheels in your area for volunteer

Facts About Older Americans

- In 2000, people age 65 and over made up 12.4 percent of the U.S. population. By 2030, this age group is expected to make up 20 percent of the U.S. population.
- People who reach the age of 65 can expect to live an additional 19 years on average.
- States with the highest percentage of people age 65 and older in 2008 were Florida (17.4 percent), West Virginia (15.7 percent), Pennsylvania (15.3 percent), Maine (15.1 percent), Iowa (14.8 percent), Hawaii (14.8 percent), North Dakota (14.7 percent), South Dakota (14.4 percent), Arkansas (14.3 percent), Montana (14.2 percent), and Rhode Island (14.1 percent).
- In 2008, 80.6 percent of Americans age 65 and over lived in metropolitan areas.
- The number of people age 85 and older is expected to increase from 4.2 million in 2000 to 6.6 million in 2020.

Source: Administration on Aging

opportunities. Another way to gain experience is to get summer or part-time work at a local hospital, nursing home, or home health care agency. Home health care aides have the opportunity to work closely with the elderly and to get to know their needs and concerns. Also, as a college student enrolled in a social work program, you may have the opportunity to help a faculty member with a geronto-logical research project.

EMPLOYERS

Opportunities for geriatric social workers can be found in both the public and private sectors. Hospitals, nursing homes, retirement communities, human services offices, senior centers, and government agencies all employ geriatric social workers. With so many services available for older people, there are a variety of job opportunities for the geriatric social worker. There are some agencies that deal only with the practical aspects of aiding older people, such as arrang-ing for services and managing financial and legal issues. Working for other agencies may involve the organization of recreational and educational activities, such as senior theater groups and art classes.

STARTING OUT

After receiving your social work degree and gaining some field expe-rience, you will have made valuable connections among faculty and social service organizations. These connections may be able to help you find a job. Your college's career services office or internship program may also direct you to your first full-time position. You should also become familiar with the local senior centers and agen-cies for the elderly.

Joining a professional organization can be helpful in entering the field. The American Society on Aging (http://www.asaging.org) sponsors a job bank and publishes newsletters. Job opportunities are listed in the newsletters and at the Web sites of the American Geri-atrics Society (http://www.americangeriatrics.org) and other profes-sional organizations. You should also attend annual meetings, which give you the chance to meet other people working in social work, geriatrics, and gerontology.

ADVANCEMENT

Most geriatric social workers enter the field focusing on the work rather than on the promotions and salary raises. However, there are advancement opportunities for dedicated social workers. Successful social workers may move up the ranks of their organizations to become supervisors or directors, taking on additional responsibilities such as overseeing new hires. A key factor in achieving the most advanced positions is to have advanced education. Those who move into the higher paid positions in administration, program development, or policy analysis must have a Ph.D. or, in some cases, a master's degree with practical experience.

Within smaller agencies and in smaller towns, advancement opportunities may be few, but there may also be less competition for these jobs. A greater number of advancement opportunities may be available in service organizations in urban areas.

EARNINGS

The U.S. Department of Labor reports that the median annual earnings of medical and public health social workers, a group that includes geriatric social workers, were $46,300 in 2009. The lowest paid 10 percent made less than $28,600, and the highest paid 10 percent made more than $71,190. Social workers working in nursing care facilities earned mean annual salaries of $43,630. Those employed in home health care services earned $49,870.

Median annual earnings for substance abuse and mental health social workers, a category that also includes geriatric social workers, were $38,200 in 2009. Salaries ranged from less than $24,940 to $62,760 or more annually.

Social workers' benefits depend on the employer, but they generally include health insurance and paid vacation time.

WORK ENVIRONMENT

Although geriatric social workers do spend some time in an office setting, they spend much of their time interviewing clients and the directors of programs; they also visit the homes of their clients to evaluate and take notes. They may also visit the homes of clients' families. Although some geriatric social workers may work in hospital and nursing home environments, others have their offices in human service agencies alongside other service providers. Serving as an advocate for the elderly client requires, in addition to phone calls, e-mails, and faxes, personal meetings with directors of agencies, local legislators, and others. In cases of abuse and neglect, it may require testifying in court.

Because poverty and illness afflict a large number of people over the age of 65, the geriatric social worker is often assigned depressing, seemingly hopeless cases. This may be the situation only temporarily, however, as the social worker introduces the client to the necessary services and assistance.

OUTLOOK

The field of social work is expected to grow much faster than the average for all careers through 2018, according to the U.S. Department of Labor (DOL). Opportunities are expected to be strongest for social workers employed in assisted-living and senior-living communities. There will also be many jobs in nursing homes, long-term care facilities, and hospices, but the DOL says employment will not be as strong in these settings because other workers are often hired to handle duties typically assigned to social workers. Those specializing in geriatric social work in particular will be in great demand for several reasons. It is estimated that as people live longer more geriatric social workers will be needed to create programs and provide services for the growing number of elderly persons. Rising health care costs are causing many insurance companies to consider alternatives to hospital treatment, so some insurance coverage now includes home stays. In addition, hospitals and nursing homes are trying to balance the demand for their services and their limitations in staff and physical facilities. As home care becomes a viable, affordable option for more older people, more geriatric social workers will be necessary to evaluate the needs of clients and set up services.

The Omnibus Budget Reconciliation Act passed by the U.S. Congress to improve nursing home care requires large nursing care facilities to employ full-time social workers. As the government becomes more involved in providing better care for the elderly, geriatric social workers will see more full-time job opportunities in nursing homes and hospitals.

FOR MORE INFORMATION

To read articles about geriatric care-related issues, visit the association's Web site.

Association for Gerontology Education in Social Work
http://www.agesw.org/

To read Careers in Aging, *visit the association's Web site.*
Association for Gerontology in Higher Education
1220 L Street, NW, Suite 901
Washington, DC 20005-4018
Tel: 202-289-9806
http://www.aghe.org

For information on licensing, contact
Association of Social Work Boards
400 South Ridge Parkway, Suite B
Culpeper, VA 22701-3791
Tel: 800-225-6880
http://www.aswb.org

For information on education and the field of social work, contact
Council on Social Work Education
1701 Duke Street, Suite 200
Alexandria, VA 22314-3457
Tel: 703-683-8080
E-mail: info@cswe.org
http://www.cswe.org

For certification information and to read Choices: Careers in Social
Work, *visit the association's Web site.*
National Association of Social Workers
750 First Street, NE, Suite 700
Washington, DC 20002-4241
Tel: 202-408-8600
http://www.naswdc.org

For more information on careers in geriatric social work, contact
American Association of Homes and Services for the Aging
2519 Connecticut Avenue, NW
Washington, DC 20008-1520
Tel: 202-783-2242
E-mail: info@aahsa.org
http://www.aahsa.org

For general information on geriatric care, contact
American Geriatrics Society
350 Fifth Avenue, Suite 801
New York, NY 10118-0801
Tel: 212-308-1414
E-mail: info@americangeriatrics.org
http://www.americangeriatrics.org

*For information on continuing education programs, job listings,
and student resources, check out the following Web site:*
American Society on Aging
71 Stevenson Street, Suite 1450
San Francisco, CA 94105-2938

Tel: 415-974-9600
E-mail: info@asaging.org
http://www.asaging.org

For career information and student resources, contact
Gerontological Society of America
1220 L Street NW, Suite 901
Washington, DC 20005-4001
Tel: 202-842-1275
http://www.geron.org

This organization can provide information on services, including adult day care, available across the country.
National Association of Area Agencies on Aging
1730 Rhode Island Avenue, NW, Suite 1200
Washington, DC 20036-3109
Tel: 202-872-0888
http://www.n4a.org

Grief Therapists

OVERVIEW

A *grief therapist* or *bereavement counselor* offers therapy for those who are mourning the death of a family member or a loved one. Therapists help survivors work through possible feelings of anger or guilt and help them recover from their loss. Counselors may be brought into communities or facilities to help individuals after a national disaster, act of violence, or an accident. Grief therapists may be self-employed as independent counselors or work for hospitals, funeral homes, schools, hospice organizations, nursing homes, or government or private agencies.

HISTORY

Grief therapy is a relatively new career specialty. According to Dr. Dana Cable, professor of psychology and thanatology at Hood College in Frederick, Maryland, and a certified grief therapist and death educator, "Grief therapy is a growing area because of the nature of many deaths today. There are many more issues to be worked through when we lose young people to violent deaths and diseases such as AIDS. In addition, there is some movement away from organized religion where people used to find comfort when they lost a loved one." Cable also points out that changes in the family unit have affected the way in which family members grieve. Many families are not close, physically or emotionally, resulting in issues of guilt when a family member dies. Other factors that have boosted growth in this field include people's willingness to accept the help of a therapist (something that rarely happened in years past) and the large number

QUICK FACTS

School Subjects
Psychology
Sociology

Personal Skills
Communication/ideas
Helping/teaching

Work Environment
Primarily indoors
One location with some
travel

Minimum Education Level
Master's degree

Salary Range
$24,230 to $38,010 to
$64,610+

Certification or Licensing
Voluntary (certification)
Required by certain states
(licensing)

Outlook
Much faster than the average

DOT
195

GOE
12.02.02

NOC
4153

O*NET-SOC
19-3031.03, 21.1014.00

Books to Read

Balk, David E., Carol Wogrin, Gordon Thornton, and David K. Meagher. (eds.) *Handbook of Thanatology: The Essential Body of Knowledge for the Study of Death, Dying, and Bereavement.* New York: Routledge, 2007.

Corr, Charles A., Clyde M. Nabe, and Donna M. Corr. *Death and Dying: Life and Living.* 6th ed. Florence, Ky.: Wadsworth Publishing, 2008.

DeSpelder, Lynne Ann, and Albert Lee Strickland. *The Last Dance: Encountering Death and Dying.* 8th ed. New York: McGraw Hill, 2008.

Worden, J. William. *Grief Counseling and Grief Therapy: A Handbook for the Mental Health Practitioner.* 4th ed. New York: Springer Publishing Company, 2008.

of aging baby boomers who are now beginning to experience the deaths of friends and family members and, thus, have a need for grief therapists' services.

THE JOB

Grief therapists help individuals accept the death of a spouse, child, partner, parent, sibling, or loved one. Therapists give their clients reassurance and help them examine and resolve feelings, including negative ones, that may be associated with the death. Counseling may be done on a one-to-one basis, with a small group, or as part of a support group.

When disasters such as accidents or violence occur, grief therapists are often brought in to speak to communities, schools, or organizations. They help people deal with the tragedy and may provide individual counseling. In recent times, therapists have been called upon when violence has hit schools, when weather-related tragedies have destroyed communities, and when an airplane has crashed or a terrorist bombing has occurred.

Hospitals, nursing homes, AIDS and cancer care centers, and hospice organizations employ grief therapists to provide emotional support to patients and their families and friends. In addition, some funeral homes refer families and friends to grief therapists as part of an aftercare service following a funeral.

Grief therapists also work as *death educators*. These specialists conduct classes for people who work in professions that deal with the sick and dying, such as medical and nursing students. They may also speak to organizations, clubs, support groups, parents, and others about issues related to death and give them suggestions on how to cope.

REQUIREMENTS
High School
College preparatory classes are essential if you wish to enter the field of grief therapy. In order to learn how to deal with a diverse group of people from all cultural backgrounds, courses in health, sociology, psychology, and religion are helpful. Communication is a key part of the grief therapist's job, so speech, foreign languages, communication, and English courses are also vital. It may be a good idea to check with the colleges you have selected to find out what courses they recommend for a career in psychology and counseling.

Postsecondary Training
Degrees that feature a strong psychology component or a premed program are usually recommended for counselors. This must be followed with a master's program in counseling, social work, or psychology. Following this with a doctoral degree in psychology is recommended for the best job prospects.

Certification or Licensing
The Association for Death Education and Counseling offers the certification in thanatology and the fellow in thanatology designations to applicants who meet educational and experiential requirements and pass a multiple-choice examination. Certification must be renewed every three years.

Some states require grief therapists to obtain licenses in order to practice. These licensing requirements may vary from state to state, so it is best to check with the state in which you plan to practice. The American Counseling Association also offers detailed information on state licensing requirements for counselors. (See For More Information.) Some states may limit counselors' private practices to areas in which they have developed professional competence. There may also be some continuing education requirements for license renewal.

Other Requirements
If you are interested in becoming a grief therapist, you should enjoy working with people and feel comfortable dealing with clients who have suffered personal loss. You should show patience and be a compassionate listener, as well as be able to express yourself clearly and tactfully.

Grief therapists must not let their jobs take an emotional toll on their own lives. Though they hear many stories of grief and sadness, therapists can also find their job rewarding and uplifting as they help people overcome feelings of depression and despair and continue with their lives.

EXPLORING

Your high school counselor may be able to supply information on a career as a therapist. Other sources for information can be found at your local or school library, or through the Internet. Contact the organizations listed at the end of this article for further information.

Doing volunteer work for organizations such as the Red Cross or with your local hospital, nursing home, or hospice care center will give you more experience dealing with the sick, troubled, or grieving. Participating in high school clubs or other groups that organize volunteer projects to benefit homeless people, victims of AIDS, or battered spouses can also give you valuable experience.

EMPLOYERS

Grief therapists may provide grief therapy as an independent part of their larger counseling practice, or they may work as part of an organization. Many therapists in private practice offer grief therapy. Some therapists are part of a group practice of medical or psychological professionals who offer a variety of counseling and therapy services. Funeral homes, nursing homes, assisted care facilities, AIDS care facilities, hospice organizations, and almost any facility or organization that deals with the sick and dying use grief therapists. Many have a therapist either on call or on staff. The government may also employ counselors and grief therapists in their health care facilities.

Some grief therapists may work under contract with large corporations as part of employee assistance programs. Others may be called upon by airlines, schools, communities, or businesses at times of crisis or when violence has occurred. They may also work on a contract basis to make presentations or seminars to various groups or organizations.

Grief therapists may also work at colleges or universities, conducting research or teaching classes that deal with death and grief.

STARTING OUT

Some colleges and universities offer job placement for people seeking careers in counseling. While in graduate school, therapy students often work as interns with hospitals, hospices, health care, or crisis care organizations, or with therapists in private practices. These relationships can often offer employment and networking possibilities after graduation.

Most grief therapists practice general counseling before specializing in grief therapy. Building a client base as a counselor can help provide the foundation for beginning a career in grief therapy. Personal contacts can also provide networking possibilities. Membership in a professional counseling association may offer sources for contacts and help you find job leads. Classified advertisements and trade magazines also list job openings.

ADVANCEMENT

Counselors specializing in grief therapy can advance to head their own counseling service or group practice, serving clients directly or contracting out services to hospitals, businesses, hospice organizations, and other facilities. Experienced grief therapists who specialize in education can become department heads of universities or colleges. Counselors with a business background and experience can advance to become executive directors of health care facilities, organizations, nursing homes, or head professional organizations that serve the counseling profession.

EARNINGS

The salary range for grief therapists is generally the same as for other therapists and counselors. According to the U.S. Department of Labor, the median annual salary of mental health counselors was $38,010 in 2009. The lowest paid 10 percent earned less than $24,230, and the highest paid 10 percent earned more than $64,610. Therapists in private practice and those who become directors of facilities may earn considerably more.

Benefits vary depending on the position and the employer but generally vacation, sick leave, insurance, and other work-related benefits are provided. Persons who are self-employed usually have to provide their own insurance and retirement funds.

WORK ENVIRONMENT

Generally, grief therapists work in office settings that are clean and well lighted. Grief therapists who work in crisis situations will find a wide variety of working environments depending on the situation, but usually small, temporary offices are set up to accommodate counselors.

Counselors in private or group practice may have to set up evening and weekend office hours. Some grief counseling must be done on an emergency basis in times of crisis or violence, so there may be occasions when counselors have to drop everything to work any time of the day or night.

Many counselors stick to a given location to serve the local community. However, depending on the type and range of cases the therapist handles, travel may be necessary, including on nights and weekends.

OUTLOOK

According to the *Occupational Outlook Handbook*, employment opportunities for mental health counselors (which includes grief therapists) are expected to grow much faster than the average for all occupations through 2018.

A career in grief therapy holds great promise. Our changing and aging society creates a need for grief counseling. As baby boomers age and experience the deaths of their parents, friends, and families, they are seeking the help of bereavement counselors to help them adjust and deal with their feelings. Counseling has become a socially accepted tool to help people deal with difficult or painful situations.

Although grief therapists work in every part of the country, demand is highest in retirement areas of the country where there is a large elderly population.

FOR MORE INFORMATION

For information on state licensing, certification, accredited graduate programs, and choosing a graduate program, contact
American Counseling Association
5999 Stevenson Avenue
Alexandria, VA 22304-3304
Tel: 800-347-6647
http://www.counseling.org

For career and certification information, contact
Association for Death Education and Counseling
111 Deer Lake Road, Suite 100
Deerfield, IL 60015-4943
Tel: 847-509-0403
http://www.adec.org

*For information on working with grieving children and their fami-
lies, contact*
The Dougy Center for Grieving Children and Families
PO Box 86852
Portland, OR 97286-0852
Tel: 866-775-5683
E-mail: help@dougy.org
http://www.grievingchild.org

For information on working with the elderly, contact
Gerontological Society of America
1220 L Street, NW, Suite 901
Washington, DC 20005-4001
Tel: 202-842-1275
http://www.geron.org

*For information on graduate programs in thanatology, or the study
of grief therapy, contact the following colleges:*
College of New Rochelle
Graduate School
29 Castle Place
New Rochelle, NY 10805-2330
Tel: 914-654-5561
E-mail: gs@cnr.edu
http://www.cnr.edu/academics/ProgramsofStudy

Hood College
401 Rosemont Avenue
Frederick, MD 21701-8524
Tel: 301-663-3131
http://www.hood.edu/graduate/programs.cfm?pid=programs_
thanatology_index.html

Health Advocates

QUICK FACTS

School Subjects
Biology
Health
Speech

Personal Skills
Communication/ideas
Helping/teaching

Work Environment
Primarily indoors
One location with some
travel

Minimum Education Level
Bachelor's degree

Salary Range
$45,000 to $60,000 to
$110,000

Certification or Licensing
None available

Outlook
About as fast as the average

DOT
N/A

GOE
N/A

NOC
N/A

O*NET-SOC
N/A

OVERVIEW

Health advocates, also known as *patient representatives* and *patient advocates,* work with and on behalf of patients to resolve issues ranging from getting insurance coverage to dealing with complaints about the medical staff to explaining a doctor's treatment plan. In addition to patients, health advocates often interact with physicians, hospitals, health maintenance organizations, insurance companies, and government agencies, to name a few. Advocates are employed by hospitals, nonprofit groups, and other health facilities, such as nursing homes. They also may work as independent contractors.

HISTORY

The world of health care has grown increasingly complex. New scientific discoveries allow doctors to better understand diseases and technology advancements that lead to new and better ways to treat patients. At the same time, government regulations, insurance company policies, hospital rules, and the legal field have all combined to make getting the appropriate health care a complicated process. It can sometimes seem as if the interests of patients get lost in the shuffle. It can be difficult for even the most informed patients to make sure they are getting the most beneficial treatment. This situation has led to the need for someone to work on behalf of patients, promoting their interests everywhere from the doctor's office to the Senate floor.

Although advocates for patients have existed for many years (some cite Florence Nightingale as the first advocate), the recognized profession of health advocate did not really begin do develop until the late 20th century. One step in this development was the acknowledgement by professionals that patients had rights and deserved quality treatment. An example of this occurred in 1973 when the American Hospital Association, a national organization representing hospitals, health care networks, and patients, adopted its first version of a Patient's Bill of Rights. Among other things, the bill recognizes that patients have the right to respectful care, the right to receive understandable information about their treatment, and the right to make their own decisions. Although the profession of health advocates was fairly small in the 1970s, its popularity has increased steadily since then, and health advocates have become important members of the health care community.

THE JOB

As insurance companies, doctors, and even the U.S. government do battle over the health care system, it can sometimes seem as if the interests of patients are being overlooked.

Because the world of health care has become so complex in recent years, it's difficult for even the most informed patients to make sure changes in the system will benefit them. Health advocates enter this struggle on the patients' behalf, using their own health care expertise to promote the interests of patients in the private and public sectors.

Primarily, there are three types of health care advocates. Those that are employed by large companies such as hospitals, insurance companies, large physician groups, and other health organizations are often called *patient representatives,* or *consumer health advocates.* The second category of health advocates works primarily for nonprofit organizations that deal with a wide variety of medical and insurance concerns, or they might work for a group that targets a particular illness or disease, such as cancer or lupus. The third group of health advocates works for private advocacy firms.

Many hospitals have seen the need and benefits of having a team devoted to resolving complaints of patients and their families and watching out for the interests of the patients as well as of the hospital. Patient representatives receive complaints from the patient or the family and work toward a resolution to the problem. The problem may range from issues between two patients sharing a room, to miscommunication between the patient and medical staff, to misplaced personal items. For example, if a patient felt mistreated by a hospital staff member, the patient representative must hear both sides of the case, determine if the claim is valid

Earn a Master's Degree in Health Advocacy

Sarah Lawrence College established the first master's degree program in health advocacy in the United States in 1980. Students must complete 48 course credits (graduate seminars and workshops), 12 fieldwork credits (600 hours in three internships), and a capstone project to earn the degree. The program typically takes four semesters and one summer to complete. Students must complete the following courses:

- Models of Advocacy: Theory and Practice
- Community Health Advocacy
- Economics of Health
- Ethics and Advocacy
- Program Design and Evaluation
- Health Care Policy
- Health Law
- History of Health Care in the United States
- Illness Narratives: Understanding the Experience of Illness
- Physiology and Disease
- Fieldwork Pro Seminar
- Capstone Pro Seminar
- Intentional Communication Pro Seminar

Visit http://www.slc.edu/graduate/programs/health-advocacy/program to learn more about this interesting program.

Source: Sarah Lawrence College

or a misunderstanding, and hopefully work out a peaceful and satisfactory resolution.

Patient representatives also document patients' concerns and experience with the hospital and its staff. Complaints and the method of resolution are recorded to help in future cases. Measuring and recording patient satisfaction are important because the hospital uses this information in finding areas to improve. Another important role of representatives is to interpret medical procedures or unfamiliar medical terms and to answer patients' questions in regards to hospital procedures or health insurance concerns. They also educate patients, as well as the hospital staff, about the patients' bill of rights, advance directives, and issues of bioethics. Sometimes they handle special religious or dietary needs of the patient or personal requests, such as commemorating a birthday.

While patient representatives work for the patients' well-being as well as their employer's best interests, health advocates employed by nonprofits act as the patient's champion against insurance companies, employers, and creditors. Many times patients are denied much-needed medical treatments because insurance companies consider them to be experimental. Certain drugs might be denied because of the way they are taken. Health advocates provide assistance in getting these issues resolved. They help identify the type of health insurance and the depth of coverage the patient has and organize paperwork and referrals from physicians and hospitals. Sometimes patients also need help composing letters to insurance companies explaining their situation. Health advocates also make phone calls to physicians and insurance companies on behalf of the patient.

Patients sometimes encounter job discrimination because of an existing illness or extended medical leaves, and this is another area in which health advocates can help. Many nonprofit groups also have lawyers on staff who provide legal counsel. Also, with any serious illness, financial concerns are likely. Health advocates can offer suggestions on how to get the most from a patient's insurance coverage, negotiate with physicians and hospitals to lower costs, and work with pharmaceutical companies in providing expensive medications at a lower cost.

Health advocates may choose to work independent of a hospital, group, or organization. Such advocates act as consultants and may have their own private practice or work for an advocacy firm. Their cases usually involve patients with a variety of issues and concerns. They usually charge a flat fee per case.

REQUIREMENTS

High School

If you are interested in working as a health advocate, take a broad range of classes in high school. Advocates need an extensive base of knowledge that covers medical, financial, emotional, and legal areas. Courses that are especially useful include business, mathematics, biology, health, and chemistry. Be sure to take four years of English as well as speech classes, because health advocates need strong oral and written communication skills. Learning a foreign language, such as Spanish, will also be useful. You may also want to take government, psychology, and computer science classes to prepare for this career.

Postsecondary Training

There is no single educational route to take to become a health advocate; the backgrounds that health advocates bring to the field tend to be as varied as their places of employment. Nevertheless, a knowledge of health care systems and medical terminology are important for you to have. Most employers prefer that you have at least a bachelor's degree. Some students choose to get degrees in health administration, premed, biology, or nursing. Helpful courses to take include communications, management, conflict resolution, and medical terminology. Some schools also offer classes in patient representation. As this profession has become more popular, schools are beginning to offer specialized programs of study. Sarah Lawrence College, for example, offers a master's degree in health advocacy. Course work for this degree includes nature of illness, position of the health advocate, health law, and ethics, as well as fieldwork.

Other Requirements

Advocates seem to agree that the most important training advocates can bring to this field is a sincere desire to work for the health and well-being of others. You can develop this commitment through community service, volunteer positions at hospitals, or caring for a loved one who has a serious illness. Though knowledge of the health care system is important, you can't do your job as an advocate unless you have the skills to convey that information in a convincing way to your audience, whether that audience is a medical ethics board or an insurance company clerk. Health advocates must be persistent and have strong problem-solving skills. Advocates must combine their medical and health administration expertise in creative ways, devising new negotiation strategies all the time. Often, obtaining the best possible outcome for patients means developing a specific plan for each new situation. Other important skills are the ability to communicate well and think analytically.

EXPLORING

One way to explore this field is by talking to people in it. Ask your school counselor to help you set up an information interview with a health advocate in your area. You may also be able to arrange to spend part of a day shadowing the advocate. Another way to learn more about this field is to learn about the issues that relate to patient advocacy. Visit your local library or surf the Internet to learn more. A good way to find out whether this field is for you is by volunteering at an organization that helps people. You might consider joining a religious group that helps the elderly or volunteering at a local hospital. Hospitals and nursing homes may also have paid part-time or summer positions available. Taking such a job will give you experience working in a health care environment and the opportunity to learn about patients' day-to-day needs. Stay up to date in this field by visiting related Web sites, such as Healthfinder.gov (http://www.healthfinder.gov).

EMPLOYERS

In addition to nonprofit organizations, private firms that specialize in patient advocacy have begun to spring up around the country. Some hospitals, specialty practices, and managed care organizations now hire patient representatives to deal with patients' complaints, and corporations supporting large health care plans for their employees have begun to do the same. Advocates working on more widespread issues in the health care industry often find employment at government agencies, community organizations, and schools developing health advocacy courses or programs.

Job descriptions for advocates may also vary significantly, depending on your place of employment. Patient representatives employed by hospitals, doctors' groups, or large corporations still work for improved health care for patients, but also they must balance their employers' interests with those of patients. For that reason, advocates at work on the insurance or treatment side of the industry may find that their jobs resemble more typical customer service positions designed to receive and resolve consumer complaints. Advocates employed by nonprofits don't have the same responsibility to consider the financial needs of the doctors and insurance companies, and they may consequently have more freedom.

STARTING OUT

Contact your college's career services office for help in finding your first job. Some hospitals advertise job openings for health advocates in the classified section of the newspaper. You may have to start out in another position in a hospital and move into health advocacy once you've gained some experience.

ADVANCEMENT

Health advocates who work as members of a staff in a hospital can advance to department manager or other administrative positions.

Some health advocates may find jobs in hospices, in AIDS programs, or with the U.S. Department of Health and Human Services.

EARNINGS

Although independent patient advocates may have more opportunities to put the patient first, they sometimes gain that freedom at the expense of job stability and a predictable salary. Patient representatives employed by hospitals, doctors' groups, and corporations can expect to earn a regular salary of $45,000 to $60,000 a year. A self-employed patient advocate or an advocate at a private firm will likely work for consultant fees that tend to vary from job to job. Some independent patient advocates charge flat fees from $75 to $150 to analyze insurance statements; if the advocate identifies any savings for the client, the advocate and client split the savings 50-50. While these rates may work out to significant earnings per year, independent advocates have no guaranteed business, and a slow year will mean a lower income. At nonprofit organizations, advocates can rely on predictable salaries; however, because nonprofits often lack the financial wherewithal of hospitals and corporations, advocates working at nonprofits tend to earn salaries at the lower end of the pay scale.

Health advocates usually receive benefits such as vacation days, sick leave, health and life insurance, and a savings and pension program.

WORK ENVIRONMENT

The type of employment that an advocate pursues largely determines their work environment. High-profile advocates striving to improve patient conditions on a national level may travel frequently, deliver speeches and seminars, and even lunch with members of Congress. Patient representatives at hospitals or managed care organizations experience a different work environment: a more standard business atmosphere, with little travel outside of the office. While it's not typical, some advocates at nonprofit or small community groups work from home. Any health advocate, though, can expect busy and varied workdays; interaction with many people is part of this job.

OUTLOOK

According to the U.S. Department of Labor, employment in the health services industry will increase as the population ages and new medical technologies evolve. In fact, the U.S. Department of Labor expects the number of jobs will increase by 22 percent between 2008 and 2018. While this figure includes all areas of health services, growth in health services is likely to contribute to health advocacy employment in the long run: as the number of patients increases and the field of health services becomes larger and more complex, patients' need for advocates can be expected to increase as well.

As the field of health advocacy grows, it most likely will become more established. New graduate programs can be expected to develop, and eventually undergraduate programs may exist as well. While the wide range of jobs available means that the field should stay diverse and deregulated, certain areas of health advocacy may develop certification procedures for their subgroups over the next five years.

FOR MORE INFORMATION

For information about education programs and to read selected articles from the Journal of the Health Advocacy Program, *contact*
Health Advocacy Program
Sarah Lawrence College
1 Mead Way
Bronxville, NY 10708-5940
Tel: 914-337-0700
http://www.slc.edu/health_advocacy

For general information about health advocacy careers, contact
Society for Healthcare Consumer Advocacy
American Hospital Association
155 North Wacker Drive, Suite 400
Chicago, IL 60606-1727
Tel: 312-422-3700
E-mail: shca@aha.org
http://www.shca-aha.org

Home Health
Care Aides

OVERVIEW

Home health care aides, also known as *homemaker-home health aides* or *home attendants,* serve elderly and infirm persons by visiting them in their homes and caring for them. Working under the supervision of nurses or social workers, they perform various household chores that clients are unable to perform for themselves as well as attend to patients' personal needs. Although they work primarily with the elderly, home health care aides also attend to clients with disabilities or those needing help with small children. There are approximately 921,700 home health aides employed in the United States.

HISTORY

Family photographs from the last century frequently included a grandparent posed alongside the children or an elderly aunt or uncle arm-in-arm with a niece or nephew. A typical household of the time often counted an elderly parent or ill or injured relative among its members. Without most of the modern conveniences we take for granted today, day-to-day living and regular household chores could be impossible for someone weakened by illness or age. It was often expected for parents to move in with children when they became unable to look after themselves; sometimes a room was prepared and waiting for them long in advance. In rural situations, elderly parents might have been expected to give up the homestead to a child or grandchild once they became incapable of looking after the place themselves.

Those without families were sometimes confined to hospitals or sanatoriums. People with contagious diseases or disabilities who required constant supervision were also cared for in institutions. Even with family, however, the needs of the elderly or infirm person often exceeded the facilities, time, and energy that the family had to offer. The business of running a household left little time for the family to tend to the needs of the terminally or seriously ill.

Rural areas often made "visiting nurses" available to check on patients who lived far from town and lacked regular transportation for medical visits. These nurses eventually discovered that the needs of the patients went beyond medical care. Patients were grateful for the company of another person in their homes, someone to read their mail to them or run errands. They were grateful not to have to abandon their own homes just because they needed a little assistance from time to time. As the demand for this kind of home care advanced, home attendants found that people needed their services, and the profession of home care aides began to grown.

Advances in modern medicine have made it possible for many illnesses to be treated at home. Hospitals and stores now rent items such as wheelchairs and oxygen tanks, enabling people to have medical equipment available in their own homes. The medical profession is also learning how a person's recovery and treatment can be affected by his or her environment. People generally recover from illnesses better when they are treated in their home environment.

The number of home care agencies has grown from about 1,100 in 1963 to more than 9,200 Medicare-certified home care agencies today.

THE JOB

Home health care aides enable elderly persons to stay in their own homes. For some clients, just a few visits a week are enough to help them look after themselves. Although physically demanding, the work is often emotionally rewarding. Home care aides may not have access to equipment and facilities such as those found in hospitals, but they also don't have the hospital's frantic pace. Home care aides are expected to take the time to get to know their clients and their individual needs. They perform their duties within the client's home environment, which often is a much better atmosphere than the impersonal rooms of a hospital.

In addition to the elderly, home health care aides assist people of any age who are recovering at home following hospitalization. They also help children whose parents are ill, disabled, or neglectful.

Aides may be trained to supply care to people suffering from specific illnesses such as AIDS, Alzheimer's disease, or cancer, or patients with developmental disabilities who lack sufficient daily living skills.

Clients unable to feed themselves may depend on home care aides to shop for food, prepare their meals, feed them, and clean up after meals. Likewise, home health care aides may assist clients in dressing and grooming, including washing, bathing, cleaning teeth and nails, and fixing the clients' hair.

Massages, alcohol rubs, whirlpool baths, and other therapies and treatments may be a part of a client's required care. Home health care aides may work closely with a physician or home nurse in giving medications and dietary supplements and helping with exercises and other therapies. They may check pulses, temperatures, and respiration rates. Occasionally, they may change nonsterile dressings, use special equipment such as a hydraulic lift, or assist with braces or artificial limbs.

Home health care aides working in home care agencies are supervised by a registered nurse, physical therapist, or social worker who assigns them specific duties. Aides report changes in patients' conditions to the supervisor or case manager.

Household chores are often another aspect of the home health care aide's responsibilities. Light housekeeping, such as changing and washing bed linens, doing the laundry and ironing, and dusting, may be necessary.

Personal attention and comfort are important aspects of an aide's care. Home health care aides can provide this support by reading to patients, playing checkers or a computer game, or visiting with an elderly client. Often just listening to a client's personal problems will help the client through the day. Because elderly people do not always have the means to venture out alone, a home health care aide may accompany an ambulatory patient to the park for an afternoon stroll or to the physician's office for an appointment.

REQUIREMENTS

High School
Many programs require only a high school diploma for entry-level positions. Previous or additional course work in family and consumer science, cooking, sewing, and meal planning are very helpful, as are courses that focus on family living and home nursing.

Postsecondary Training
Health care agencies usually focus their training on first aid, hygiene, and the principles of health care. Cooking and nutrition, including

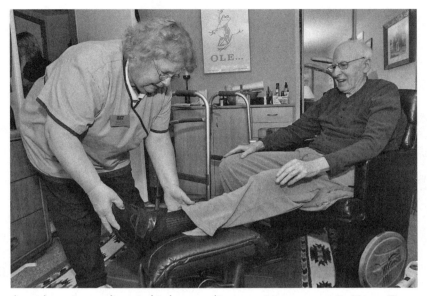

An aide assists a client in his home. *(Syracuse Newspapers, D. Blume, The Image Works)*

meal preparation for patients with specific dietary needs, are often included in the program. Home health care aides may take courses in psychology and child development as well as family living. Because of the need for hands-on work, aides usually learn how to bathe, dress, and feed patients as well as how to help them walk upstairs or get up from bed. The more specific the skill required for certain patients, the more an agency is likely to have more comprehensive instruction.

Most agencies will offer training to prospective employees. Such training may include instruction on how to deal with depressed or reluctant patients, how to prepare easy and nutritious meals, and tips on housekeeping. Specific course work on health and sanitation may also be required.

Certification or Licensing

Home Care University, a subsidiary of the National Association for Home Care and Hospice, offers the home care aide certification to applications who complete educational and skill requirements and pass a written examination. Contact the association for more information.

The federal government has enacted guidelines for home health aides whose employers receive reimbursement from Medicare. Federal law requires home health aides to pass a competency test covering 12 areas: communication skills; documentation of patient status and care provided; reading and recording vital signs; basic infection control procedures; basic body functions; maintenance of a healthy environment; emergency procedures; physical, emotional, and developmental characteristics of patients; personal hygiene and grooming; safe transfer techniques; normal range of motion and positioning; and basic nutrition.

Federal law suggests at least 75 hours of classroom and practical training supervised by a registered nurse. Training and testing programs may be offered by the employing agency, but they must meet the standards of the Centers for Medicare and Medicaid Services. Training programs vary depending upon state regulations.

Other Requirements

Caring for people in their own homes can be physically demanding work. Lifting a client for baths and exercise, helping a client up and down stairs, performing housework, and aiding with physical therapy all require that an aide be in good physical condition. Aides do not have the equipment and facilities of a hospital to help them with their work, and this requires adaptability and ingenuity. Oftentimes they must make do with the resources available in a typical home.

An even temperament and a willingness to serve others are important characteristics for home health care aides. People in this occupation should be friendly, patient, sensitive to others' needs, and tactful. At times an aide will have to be stern in dealing with uncooperative patients or calm and understanding with those who are angry, confused, despondent, or in pain. Genuine warmth and respect for others are important attributes. Cheerfulness and a sense of humor can go a long way in establishing a good relationship with a client, and a good relationship can make working with the client much easier.

Home health care aides must be willing to follow instructions and abide by the health plan created for each patient. Aides provide an important outreach service, supporting the care administered by the patient's physician, therapist, or social worker. They are not trained medical personnel, however, and must know the limits of their authority.

EXPLORING

Home health care aides are employed in many different areas. Interested students can learn more about the work by contacting local agencies and programs that provide home care services and requesting information on the organization's employment guidelines or training programs. Visiting the county or city health department and contacting the personnel director may provide useful information as well. Often, local organizations sponsor open houses to inform the community about the services they provide. This could serve as an excellent opportunity to meet the staff involved in hiring and program development and to learn about job opportunities. In addition, it may be possible to arrange to accompany a home health care aide on a home visit.

EMPLOYERS

Approximately 921,700 home health care aides are employed in the United States. The primary employers of home health care aides are local social service agencies that provide home care services. Such agencies often have training programs for prospective employees. Home health care aides might also find employment with hospitals that operate their own community outreach programs. Most hospitals, however, hire home health care aides through agencies.

STARTING OUT

Some social service agencies enlist the aid of volunteers. By contacting agencies and inquiring about such openings, aspiring home care aides can get an introduction to the type of work this profession requires. Also, many agencies or nursing care facilities offer training to prospective employees.

Checking the local Yellow Pages for agencies that provide health care to the aged and disabled or family service organizations can provide a list of employment prospects. Nursing homes, public and private health care facilities, and local chapters of the Red Cross and United Way are likely to hire entry-level employees. The National Association for Home Care and Hospice can also supply information on reputable agencies and departments that employ home care aides.

ADVANCEMENT

As home health care aides develop their skills and deepen their experience, they may advance to management or supervisory positions. Those who find greater enjoyment working with clients may branch into more specialized care and pursue additional training. Additional experience and education often bring higher pay and increased responsibility.

Aides who wish to work in a clinic or hospital setting may return to school to complete a nursing degree. Other related occupations include social worker, physical or occupational therapist, and dietitian. Along with a desire for advancement, however, must come the willingness to meet additional education and experience requirements.

EARNINGS

Earnings for home health care aides are comparable to the salaries of nursing and psychiatric aides and nurse assistants. Depending on the agency, considerable flexibility exists in working hours and patient load. For many aides who begin as part-time employees, the starting salary is usually the minimum hourly wage ($7.25). For full-time aides with significant training or experience, earnings may be around $8 to $11 per hour. According to the U.S. Department of Labor (DOL), median hourly earnings of home health aides were $9.85 in 2009. The most experienced home health care aides earned more than $14.13 an hour. The DOL reported annual salaries in 2009 for aides working a regular 40-hour week ranged from less than $15,950 to $29,390 or more, with a median salary of $20,480.

Aides are usually paid only for the time worked in the home. They normally are not paid for travel time between jobs.

Vacation policies and benefits packages vary with the type and size of the employing agency. Many full-time home health care aides receive one week of paid vacation following their first year of employment, and they often receive two weeks of paid vacation each year thereafter. Full-time aides may also be eligible for health insurance and retirement benefits. Some agencies also offer holiday or overtime compensation.

WORK ENVIRONMENT

Health aides in a hospital or nursing home setting work at a much different pace and in a much different environment than the home health care aide. With home care, aides can take the time to sit with their clients and get to know them. Aides spend a certain amount of time with each client and can perform their responsibilities without the frequent distractions and demands of a hospital. Home surroundings differ from situation to situation. Some homes are neat and pleasant, while others are untidy and depressing. Some patients are angry, abusive, depressed, or otherwise difficult; others are pleasant and cooperative.

Because home health care aides usually have more than one patient, the hours an aide works can fluctuate based on the number of clients and types of services needed. Many clients may be ill or have disabilities. Some may be elderly and have no one else to assist them with light housekeeping or daily errands. These differences can dictate the type of responsibilities a home care aide has for each patient.

Working with the infirm or disabled can be a rewarding experience as aides enhance the quality of their clients' lives with their help and company. However, the personal strains—on the clients as well as the aides—can make the work challenging and occasionally frustrating. There can be difficult emotional demands that aides may find exhausting. Considerable physical activity is involved in this line of work, such as helping patients to walk, dress, or take care of themselves. Traveling from one home to another and running various errands for patients can also be tiring and time consuming, or it can be a pleasant break.

OUTLOOK

As government and private agencies develop more programs to assist the dependent, the need for home health care aides will continue to grow. Because of the physical and emotional demands of the job, there is high turnover and, therefore, frequent job openings for home health care aides.

Also, the number of people 65 years of age and older is expected to increase substantially, and many of them will require at least some home care. Rising health care costs are causing many insurance companies to consider alternatives to hospital treatment, so many insurance providers now cover home care services. In addition, hospitals and nursing homes are trying to balance the demand for their services and their limitations in staff and physical facilities. The availability of home health care aides can allow such institutions as hospitals and nursing homes to offer quality care to more people. The U.S. Department of Labor projects that employment of home health aides will grow by 50 percent through 2018, or much faster than the average for all occupations.

FOR MORE INFORMATION

For information on caring for the elderly, contact
ElderWeb
1305 Chadwick Drive
Normal, IL 61761
Tel: 309-451-3319
E-mail: info@elderweb.com
http://www.elderweb.com

For certification information and statistics on the home health care industry, visit the association's Web site.

National Association for Home Care and Hospice
228 Seventh Street, SE
Washington, DC 20003-4306
Tel: 202-547-7424
http://www.nahc.org

Hospice Workers

OVERVIEW

Hospice workers provide support for terminally ill patients in the final stages of their illness. Hospice care is a benefit under Medicare Hospital Insurance and eligible persons can receive medical and support services for their terminal illnesses. Care is primarily provided in the patients' homes, but may also be provided in nursing homes and hospitals, with the intent to make patients as comfortable and pain-free as medically possible during the final days of their lives. A team of specially trained professionals and volunteers provides hospice care. The National Hospice and Palliative Care Organization estimates that 1.45 million patients are served by hospice organizations each year.

HISTORY

The hospice concept can be traced to ancient times when shelter and rest (hospitality) were provided for travelers. Home care has also been a tradition in America since the 1880s when public health nurses began traveling to patients' homes to care for the sick and comfort the dying. However, the term hospice was first used in 1967 to mean specialized care for dying patients when St. Christopher's Hospice in a residential suburb of London was established. The first hospice in the United States, The Connecticut Hospice, was established in 1974. Today, hospice refers to a type of compassionate care and support given to the dying patient and to the patient's family and caregivers. There are approximately 4,850 organizations that provide hospice services in the United States.

THE JOB

Hospice workers help patients who have a variety of terminal illnesses and who can no longer benefit from curative treatment. Typically, a hospice patient has less than six months to live.

Hospice workers are a team of trained professionals that include administrators, physicians, nurses, counselors, chaplains, therapists, social workers, aides, and volunteers. Hospice organizations rely heavily on volunteers, who must participate in intensive volunteer training. According to a study by the National Hospice and Palliative Care Association of America, in 2008, more than 550,000 hospice volunteers in the United States provided 25 million hours of service.

Hospices use a team approach to plan and coordinate care for the patient. This team includes the patient, family, and the hospice team, all working together. Family or primary caregivers can call for the help of a hospice team member 24 hours a day, seven days a week, and a team member will respond whenever needed.

Hospice workers' job responsibilities are related to their profession. *Hospice medical directors* may be licensed physicians who oversee the medical program and advise the hospice care staff. *Registered nurses* may be responsible for seeing that a member of the hospice team meets the patient's needs. Nurses also visit patients to monitor their emotional and physical symptoms. *Nurse assistants* and *home health care aides* assist the family in the personal care of the patient such as bathing, grooming, and changing the bed linens. *Physical, occupational,* and *speech therapists* help patients with daily living tasks that have become difficult or impossible to perform. *Social workers* help the patient and family deal with the emotions surrounding the illness. They also help locate personal and community resources that may assist the patient or the family. *Volunteer coordinators* organize and direct the volunteer program and for training the volunteer workers. *Chaplains* provide religious support to the patient and family in accordance with their specific religious beliefs. *Music therapists* use music to provide comfort and relaxation to the patient. *Grief therapists* help the family deal with the death of their loved one and cope with their grief.

REQUIREMENTS

High School

Persons wishing to obtain a college degree in one of the professions employed by hospice organizations should take a well-balanced college preparatory course in high school, with a good foundation in the sciences. Biology, chemistry, and psychology are important courses.

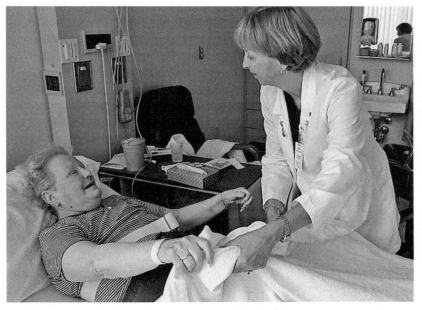

A hospice nurse helps a patient get out of bed. *(Michael Reigner, AP Photo)*

You should take anatomy and physiology if your high school offers these courses. You should also take courses in the humanities and social sciences, as well as classes that improve communication skills.

High school diploma requirements vary with hospice organizations and the volunteer responsibilities. Some volunteer work for example, answering the phones, cleaning, or maintaining grounds, does not require a diploma of any kind. However, a high school diploma would probably be required for any volunteer position that involves patient contact.

Postsecondary Training
The degree program you should pursue depends on the role you hope to play in the hospice programs. Some positions require a bachelor's degree and others a medical degree or other specialized degree. Many hospitals offer medical rotations in hospice care to physicians, nurses, and other professionals involved in training. Madonna University in Livonia, Michigan, offers the only university-based hospice and palliative studies program of study in the United States. Visit http://www. madonna.edu/pages/hospiceeducation.cfm for more information.

Certification or Licensing
The certification or licensing requirements are determined by the medical specialty or professional career that you wish to pursue. The

hospice itself is usually licensed by the department of health of each state (more than 40 states license hospice programs) and certified by Medicare and Medicaid. Additionally, the National Association for Home Care and Hospice offers certification for home care aides and hospice executives. Contact the association for more information.

Other Requirements

If you are planning to become involved in hospice care, you should be able to work as a member of a team to provide the support and care that is needed by terminally ill patients and their loved ones and caregivers. You should be compassionate, patient, sensitive, and well organized. Flexibility and the ability to make decisions are important. You should also feel comfortable dealing with the sick and dying.

EXPLORING

There are many ways to learn more about a career as a hospice worker. You can read books and magazines about hospice care. There are also many Web sites that discuss the career and issues in the field. Visit the Web sites of the professional associations at the end of this article. Ask a teacher or counselor to arrange an information interview with a hospice worker. You also can volunteer to care for a family member who is ill or elderly or volunteer at a local hospice or social services agency.

EMPLOYERS

Hospice organizations hire hospice workers and also welcome hospice volunteers. As of 2008, there were approximately 4,850 hospice programs in all 50 states, the District of Columbia, and Puerto Rico. About 57 percent of these hospices operated as independent entities, while others were associated with hospitals, home health agencies, and nursing facilities. About 50 percent of hospices are nonprofit organizations.

STARTING OUT

If you are interested in pursuing a career as a hospice worker, you should consider doing volunteer work at a hospice center, hospital, or nursing home when in high school. This will give you an insight into the hospice environment and its career possibilities.

If you choose to complete professional training, a career services office associated with your degree program may help you locate employment opportunities. In addition, contacts you made in clinical settings while training or volunteering may be helpful. Applying directly to hospices and other health care agencies and answering ads in professional journals can also produce employment opportunities.

ADVANCEMENT

Advancement opportunities include director and supervisor positions within the hospice program. Other career opportunities may exist with government agencies and organizations associated with hospice and home health care programs. A degree may be required to advance to some positions.

EARNINGS

Salaries for hospice workers are similar to those of their counterparts in a more typical medical setting and generally are based on the position, the educational requirements for that position, and the level of experience of the worker. According to the *2008–09 Hospice Salary and Benefits Report* conducted by the Hospital and Healthcare Compensation Service in cooperation with the Hospice Association of America, salaries for directors of hospice ranged from $76,005 to $101,944. Salaries for directors of social work and counseling ranged from $54,100 to $72,100, while directors of clinical services earned $67,124 to $85,700. The Hospital and Healthcare Compensation Service and the Hospice Association of America report the following hourly salary ranges for hospice professionals by job specialty: registered nurse, $24.23 to $28.50; licensed practical nurse, $16.83 to $20.76; physical therapist, $31.62 to $36.50; social worker (with a master's degree in social work), $20.55 to $24.89; and director of volunteer services, $16.37 to $21.84.

Hospice chaplains, music therapists, and grief therapists may earn salaries that range from $20,000 to $40,000 or more annually.

Fringe benefits are usually similar to those of other full-time health care workers and may include sick leave, vacation, health and life insurance, and tuition assistance.

WORK ENVIRONMENT

Most hospice workers visit terminally ill patients in their homes or in the homes of their caregivers so the work environment can be as varied as their patients' lifestyles. Some workers are on call 24 hours a day and may be required to travel to homes in all areas of a city or rural area to provide medical and supportive care. Patients and family members can be very tense during this stressful period in their lives, and they may be unpleasant and uncooperative at times. As with any health care profession, hospice workers have the possibility of exposure to contagious diseases; however, proper precautions and training diminish this risk.

OUTLOOK

Hospice participation has grown at a dramatic rate, especially among those involved with Medicare. According to the National Association for Home Care and Hospice, from 1984 to 2008 the total number of hospices participating in Medicare rose from 31 to 3,257—a nearly 105-fold increase. The number of hospices and patients serviced by them is expected to increase as the population ages and health care costs rise. In addition, families and medical professionals are choosing hospice care because of its holistic, patient-family, in-home-centered philosophy.

FOR MORE INFORMATION

For information on hospice care, contact
Hospice Education Institute
3 Unity Square
PO Box 98
Machiasport, ME 04655-0098
Tel: 800-331-1620
E-mail: info@hospiceworld.org
http://www.hospiceworld.org

For general information about hospice care, contact
National Association for Home Care and Hospice
228 Seventh Street, SE
Washington, DC 20003-4306
Tel: 202-547-7424
http://www.nahc.org

For industry statistics, contact
National Hospice and Palliative Care Organization
1731 King Street, Suite 100
Alexandria, VA 22314-2720
Tel: 703-837-1500
E-mail: nhpco_info@nhpco.org
http://www.nhpco.org

fraternal or religious groups. Proprietary facilities are those run for profit by individuals, partnerships, or corporations. And government facilities are run, of course, by the government and include such places as veterans' homes and state-run nursing homes.

However, no matter what type of facility they work for and no matter who owns the facility, all nursing home administrators are responsible for every aspect of maintaining and operating that home. Their many duties range from management of personnel to public relations. Depending on the size of the facility, administrators may have one or more assistants to help with the daily responsibilities.

If the nursing home is part of a large corporation, the administrator must meet with the governing board or other administrators from different facilities within the company. They take an active role in helping plan budgets and programs. For example, if staff resources are low or new equipment or remodeling is needed, the administrator must explain the situation to the corporate office in order to get proper funding for the project. They may also help set fee schedules for patient services.

Administrators oversee every department in the nursing home from dietary to medical records. Some departments may have their own managers, but these managers must report to the administrator. Many times, administrators interview and hire department managers; they also have a voice in how staff members are trained and supervised. Administrators also work with the medical director and nursing director to plan medical policies and procedures that will ensure the best health care for all the residents. They also work with the activities director in planning recreational events, holiday parties, and other year-round entertainment for the residents.

Administrators are responsible for dealing with different government agencies that monitor health care. Nursing homes must meet strict guidelines before becoming Medicare and/or Medicaid certified by the federal agency Centers for Medicare and Medicaid Services (CMS). Without CMS approval, Medicare and Medicaid will not pay for any services rendered at the facility. In addition, every nursing home facility undergoes an annual inspection by the state's health department. Any discrepancies or violations found are directed to the administrator for explanation. Many nursing homes also participate in voluntary quality assurance programs that measure the performance of the facility and its staff.

If there are problems with the staff, or complaints regarding a client's treatment or well-being, the administrator must intervene. A good administrator should be able to listen, assess the situation, and act accordingly. Administrators should not only be visible to patients and their families, but be approachable as well.

REQUIREMENTS

High School

Are you thinking about a career in health administration? If you are, you should know that there are several key classes to include in your high school curriculum. Managing a nursing home is very similar to managing a business. Classes such as accounting, business management, and computer science will help prepare you for the business side of this job. Quantitative skills are needed to excel in this career, so make sure you take as many math classes as possible. Science and health classes are important to take and will prepare you for college. High school classes in sociology, psychology, and social studies can provide you with a background for understanding a variety of people. And, because you will be working with so many different people and must give directions, take English, speech, and foreign language classes to hone your communication and leadership skills.

Postsecondary Training

Most nursing home administrators have a college degree in health administration, business, human resources, or another related field. A few states do allow licensing for administrators who hold an associate's degree and have a certain amount of experience. It is recommended, however, that you get a bachelor's degree. One reason for this is that requirements for professional certification stipulate that

Words to Know

adult home: senior citizens' home that provides meals, personal care services, and private or semiprivate rooms, but no medical services

assisted living: combines enriched housing and nursing care services

congregate care: general term for senior citizen housing with some care services

enriched housing: an adult home with individual apartments and no personal care services

independent living: housing for the well elderly, which may include housekeeping and some meal services; housing may be apartments, cottages, condos, etc.

life care retirement community: provides the full range of living options for the elderly, from independent living to nursing homes

Source: Health Advocates for Older People Inc.

anyone licensed must also hold a bachelor's degree to be eligible for certification. In addition, most employers insist on hiring only those with at least a bachelor's degree.

Many colleges and universities across the United States offer bachelor's degrees in health care administration, health service administration, or long-term care administration with concentrations or minors in nursing home management. The Association of University Programs in Health Administration certifies undergraduate and graduate programs that meet the organization's standards. The National Association of Long Term Care Administrator Boards grants academic approval to undergraduate programs in long-term care administration. The Commission on Accreditation of Healthcare Management Education is the accrediting body for graduate programs in health administration education. Graduates of advanced-degree programs usually have a master's of science in health administration or a master's in business administration in health care management.

Courses you are likely to take as an undergraduate cover subjects such as health law, gerontology, medical terminology, and health care financial management. In addition, expect to take classes such as accounting, marketing, computer science, and organizational theory. Some programs also require students to complete an internship, also called an administrator-in-training program.

Certification or Licensing
Professional certification is available from the American College of Health Care Administrators. Certification requirements include having a bachelor's degree, having two years of professional experience as a nursing home administrator, completing a certain amount of continuing education, and passing the certification exam. Candidates who meet all requirements receive the designation certified nursing home administrator. The certified assisted living administrator designation is also available. Certification demonstrates an administrator's level of experience and professionalism and is recommended. The American College of Healthcare Executives (ACHE) offers the certified healthcare executive designation to candidates who pass an examination and meet other requirements. Fellow status is available to certified healthcare executives with advanced experience and skills. Contact the ACHE for more information.

All nursing home administrators must be licensed. All states and the District of Columbia require candidates to pass a national licensing exam given by the National Association of Long Term Care Administrator Boards. In addition, many states require candidates to pass a state exam as well as to fulfill certain requirements, such as having completed an administrator-in-training program of a certain length and completing a certain number of continuing education hours. Since these state requirements vary, you will need to check with the licensing board of the state in which you hope to work for specific information.

Other Requirements

Nursing home administrators must have a keen sense for business and enjoy managing people, budgets, and resources. They should be able to work well with a wide variety of people, from government officials to residents' families. But just as important as having a feel for business, nursing home administrators must have a special interest in helping people, especially the elderly. Administrators need to be aware of the emotional and physical challenges their residents face and be able to figure out ways to make their facilities accommodating. Administrators need to have a positive attitude and to be committed to lifelong learning, since continuing education is an essential part of this work.

EXPLORING

To explore the field of nursing home administration, try contacting a nursing home in your area and make an appointment to speak with the administrator or assistant administrator about this work. They should be able to answer any questions you may have about the job, as well as give you a feel for their workday.

Hands-on experience is also important, so volunteer at a local nursing home or assisted living residence. You can help conduct activities such as games, arts and crafts, holiday celebrations, reading aloud to the sight impaired, or simply keeping lonely seniors company. Most, if not all, facilities welcome volunteers. In addition, there may be opportunities for paid part-time or summer jobs at these facilities. Even if you end up only working in the kitchen, you will still get a good feel for the structure of the business.

EMPLOYERS

There are about 16,000 nursing homes located throughout the United States. Each nursing home, depending on its size, needs administrators and assistant administrators to oversee its operation. Nonprofit groups, corporations, and government agencies employ administrators in a variety of settings: at skilled nursing, intermediate care, and residential facilities. No matter what the facility is, however, each needs administrative leadership to ensure successful operation.

Job opportunities vary from state to state. According to the Administration on Aging, California had the largest number of residents age 65 and over in 2009, with approximately 4.1 million. Other states with large populations of elderly people were Florida (3.2 million), New York (2.6 million), Texas (2.5 million), and Pennsylvania (1.9 million). Alaska, on the other hand, ranked at the bottom with approximately 50,277 residents in this age group. It makes sense to conclude that opportunities for nursing home employment are most plentiful in areas with high concentrations of older residents.

STARTING OUT

A nursing home administrator is considered a high executive position, so it is quite rare to land this job directly after graduation. Working as an assistant administrator is a more realistic mid-level management position. It is not uncommon for administrators to have one or more assistants responsible for different aspects of running the nursing home, especially at larger facilities. For example, one assistant administrator may be in charge of human resources and benefits, while another is assigned to keeping inventory and purchasing supplies. The administrator oversees the work of each assistant.

As a starting point for the career of administrator, however, you may begin as an activity director or, depending on the size of the facility, as an assistant to the activity director. Nursing home patients look forward to a variety of diversions to help make their stay pleasant and enjoyable. Coordinating weekly patient entertainment, such as bingo games, arts and crafts, holiday parties, and other celebrations, are some of the duties of an activity director.

Other routes into this field include jobs that familiarize you with government agencies and case management.

ADVANCEMENT

It is hard to identify a typical route of advancement for the nursing home administrator, since this is already considered an executive position. Experienced administrators might choose to work for a larger nursing home with a bigger staff. If employed by a chain, administrators may advance by being transferred to other nursing home locations or promoted to the corporate office. Administrative positions at hospitals, health maintenance organizations, pharmaceutical companies, or national associations, such as the Red Cross, are other options for advancement. The skills and experience nursing home administrators possess, such as management and budgeting, can be easily applied to other areas of the corporate world.

EARNINGS

The U.S. Department of Labor reports that medical and health services managers working at nursing care facilities earned mean annual salaries of $77,560 in 2009. Salaries for all medical and health services managers ranged from less than $49,750 to $140,300 or more. These salaries do not include bonuses. Income also depends on the administrator's experience, the size of the facility, its ownership, and its location.

Administrators receive added benefits such as health and life insurance, paid vacation and sick time, and retirement plans.

WORK ENVIRONMENT

Most administrators are scheduled for eight-hour workdays, although they often work longer hours, especially when there are a large number of admissions or if there is a problem that needs to be addressed. Administrators must be available at all hours to handle any emergency that may arise. Most keep a regular Monday through Friday work schedule; some work on weekends.

Administrators usually have private offices, but the nature of their job takes them to every department and floor of the nursing home facility. If there is a problem in the dietary department, the administrator must go to the dietitian's office or the kitchen. A resident's complaint may take the administrator to that particular room.

Most nursing home facilities do not enforce a dress code for nonmedical staff. However, it is important to dress professionally and in a manner appropriate to the environment.

OUTLOOK

Nursing home administration, like many careers in geriatric care, is a field to watch. Employment of health service managers is expected to grow faster than the average for all careers through 2018, according to the U.S. Department of Labor. Much of the anticipated employment opportunities will be at nursing homes and other residential facilities.

One reason for this demand will be the increased number of seniors. The Administration on Aging projects there will be approximately 71.5 million older persons, age 65 years or older, by 2030. This age group will grow dramatically as more of the baby boom generation (those born from the mid-1940s to the mid-1960s) reach senior status.

People are also living longer than ever before due to improvements in medical care and healthier lifestyles. As life expectancies rise, many families are presented with the unique situation of caring for their elderly parents, and sometimes their grandparents, while raising their own young families.

Another reason nursing home facilities and those who work in them will be in demand is our mobile society. People relocate today much more than in generations past, often moving away from their original homes for better employment opportunities. It is not uncommon for the elderly to have no immediate family members living close by. The primary reason many senior citizens enter nursing homes is their inability to care for themselves due to chronic illness or advanced age. According to a study conducted by Columbia University's College of Physicians and Surgeons, the "typical" nursing home resident's stay is two and a half years. As the number of people requiring round-the-clock medical attention increases, so will the need for more nursing home facilities. This, in turn, will fuel a demand for qualified nursing home administrators.

FOR MORE INFORMATION

For information regarding nonprofit facilities, contact
American Association of Homes and Services for the Aging
2519 Connecticut Avenue, NW
Washington, DC 20008-1520
Tel: 202-783-2242
E-mail: info@aahsa.org
http://www.aahsa.org

For information on careers, certification, and licensure, contact the following organizations:
American College of Health Care Administrators
1321 Duke Street, Suite 400
Alexandria, VA 22314-3563
Tel: 202-536-5120
http://www.achca.org

American College of Healthcare Executives
One North Franklin Street, Suite 1700
Chicago, IL 60606-3529
Tel: 312-424-2800
http://www.ache.org

For information regarding long-term health care and its facilities in the United States, contact
American Health Care Association
1201 L Street, NW

Washington, DC 20005-4024
Tel: 202-842-4444
http://www.ahca.org

Contact the AUPHA for information regarding accredited academic programs in health administration.
Association of University Programs in Health Administration (AUPHA)
2000 North 14th Street, Suite 780
Arlington, VA 22201-2543
Tel: 703-894-0940
E-mail: aupha@aupha.org
http://www.aupha.org

For information on graduate programs in health administration education, contact
Commission on Accreditation of Healthcare Management Education
2111 Wilson Boulevard, Suite 700
Arlington, VA 22201-3052
Tel: 703-351-5010
E-mail: info@cahme.org
http://www.cahme.org

For information on licensing and undergraduate degree programs in long-term care administration, visit the association's Web site.
National Association of Long Term Care Administrator Boards
1444 I Street, NW
Washington, DC 20005-6542
Tel: 202-712-9040
E-mail: nab@nabweb.org
http://www.nabweb.org

For information on education and licensing, visit
Long Term Care Education
http://www.longtermcareeducation.com

For information on a career as a health care executive, visit
Make a Difference...Discover a Career in Healthcare Management
http://www.healthmanagementcareers.com

═══ **INTERVIEW** ═══

Helen Lacek is the owner (along with her husband) of Oakridge Nursing Home and Rehab Center, a 70-bed facility in Hillside,

Illinois. Her husband serves as the chief financial officer of the business, and Helen is the administrator and oversees the daily operation of the facility. Helen discussed her career with the editors of Careers in Focus: Geriatric Care.

Q. What made you want to become a nursing home administrator?

A. Twenty-seven years ago, I got laid off at a Veterans Administration hospital, and was only able to find employment—as a licensed practical nurse—at a local nursing home. I quickly fell in love with the whole makeup of a nursing home. Because I was a hard worker, I was promoted fairly quickly. I started out as a floor nurse. From there I was promoted to supervisor, then to program coordinator, then to assistant administrator. I was then promoted to director of nursing, and then became an administrator. Soon I was managing up to seven homes at one time.

Q. What do you like the most about your career?

A. I like knowing I can make a difference in someone's life. Besides the patient, I also become close to their family members, and help them transition to this part of life. We are the ones who see the elderly at their worst, and help their families during that time. There may be some difficult situations when dealing with family members, but it's important to be able to listen to all sides. Being patient definitely can help calm the waters.

Q. What do you like the least?

A. Definitely the paperwork. Also, being the owner of a facility can translate to long hours, 24 hours a day, seven days a week—but I don't mind so much.

Another burden, especially in my capacity, is cash flow. We often have to wait long periods of time for payment for services rendered—even though I am still expected to offer all services and equipment needed, as well as salaries for my staff and maintain the building.

Q. What are some important skills or personal qualities needed to become a nursing home administrator?

A. People skills are definitely important. Also, students should be ready to roll up their sleeves—the days of administrators sitting behind an office desk are over. Knowing all aspects of the business is the only way the operation will be successful.

It's also important for students to be able to learn from their mistakes. Don't take mistakes as failure, but rather an opportunity to become better in your job.

It makes sense that many administrators have a background in nursing—it certainly helps when running a nursing home. However, many nurses may have difficulty with the business aspect of the job.

There are several programs available that award certification in nursing home administration. Many colleges also offer a four-year degree in health care administration. I feel, however, that in the field of long-term care, it's not so much what you bring to the table—meaning your degree or education—but rather your abilities. It's important to be able to be a chameleon in many situations and be able to adapt according to these different situations. One thing I have discovered in my years working in long-term care is that if you work hard and show interest in what you are doing, you'll go far.

Q. What advice would you give students who are interested in this career?

A. I would advise students to get as much varied experience as possible. This could mean working in the cafeteria doing dishes, or perhaps working in the laundry and supply department, even helping making hospital beds. Know as many jobs as possible. Volunteering at a nursing home is a great way to gain experience. In fact, I have many high school students who volunteer at my facility as a way to accrue community service hours needed for graduation. There may also be opportunities for students to work at a nursing home, but only in positions that do not involve direct patient care.

Q. What is the future employment outlook for nursing home administrators?

A. There is definitely a positive outlook for this field. The baby boomers are getting older and people are living longer. Many nursing home administrators also branch out into other patient care opportunities such as home health and assisted living.

Orientation and Mobility Specialists

OVERVIEW

Orientation and mobility specialists help people with disabilities stay actively involved in society. They teach blind, visually impaired, and disabled individuals how to master the skills necessary to live independently and often encourage them to participate in various educational or recreational programs. Specialists also serve as a source of information, referring clients to financial aid, benefits, and legal advice. These workers may be employed directly by an individual or indirectly through community planning, research, and publicity projects.

HISTORY

Helping those with disabilities has long been a part of the social work profession. As early as 1657, facilities called almshouses provided shelter, food, and work to the poor and those with disabilities. In the mid-1800s, middle-class women referred to as "friendly visitors" visited the homes of poor families to instruct the disabled in household management, the pursuit of employment, and the education of children. However, these friendly visitors and other early charitable organizations were sometimes limited in whom they would serve, often providing help and information only to those with their same moral views and religious backgrounds.

People with severe disabilities were often confined to institutions. By the late 18th century, many states and counties had built these facilities, then referred to as insane asylums, for the 24-hour care of people suffering from afflictions ranging from mental retardation to paralysis. The patients of these hospitals were often committed against their will by relatives. Few efforts were made to help patients return to society to lead normal, active lives.

The settlement houses of the late 19th century, such as Jane Addams's Hull House of Chicago, led to the development of more sensitive and enlightened ways to help people. Social workers lived among the residents, listening and learning along with them. But even with this new understanding of social work, those with disabilities were still unable to get complete assistance. Society wanted to help those in need but didn't necessarily want to live among them. As a result, separate schools, workplaces, and agencies for the disabled were established. Although social workers instructed blind people in how to cook and clean, how to use a guide dog, and how to read braille, they made few efforts to integrate them into the community.

Legal efforts to end this discrimination began in 1920 with the passing of the Vocational Rehabilitation Act. This act led to the development of state and federal agencies focused on enhancing the employment opportunities for people with disabilities. Over the years, this act has broadened to include job counseling and retraining services and the provision of prosthetic and other assisting devices. More recent efforts toward ending discrimination in employment and public services include the passing of the Americans with Disabilities Act of 1990.

THE JOB

Although he was diagnosed with multiple sclerosis years ago, Ken has only recently required the use of a wheelchair. He also has only partial use of his right hand. Despite being several years past the traditional retirement age, Ken works as a newspaper journalist for a local newspaper. He loves his job. In the past, he drove himself to crime scenes, took notes during interviews, and wrote at a frantic pace to keep up with the pace of the newsroom. Now that he requires a wheelchair to get around, he is going to have to make many adjustments in his life. Fortunately for Ken, there are a number of services and benefits to help him; he just needs to know how to find this help.

The simple act of providing information is one of the most important jobs of an orientation and mobility specialist. These workers help to direct people like Ken to the many agencies available that assist those with vision and mobility impairments. By listening carefully to the problem, orientation and mobility specialists determine the best route for assistance, contact the agency on behalf of the client, and make sure the client receives the proper assistance. Because of limited funding and support, disability services are often unable to promote themselves. The biggest problem facing communities is not the lack of services available, but the lack of public awareness of these outlets.

However, Ken will require much more than names and phone numbers from an orientation and mobility specialist. He not only needs to find the right wheelchair, but he also needs instruction on how to use it. His home needs to be analyzed to determine what modifications need to be made (for example, wheelchair ramps, handrails, and wider doorways). If the necessary modifications cannot be made, he will have to consider moving to a new place. For all of these somewhat daunting decisions, Ken can ask an orientation and mobility specialist for advice.

Ken's workplace may also require modifications. Though perfectly capable of continuing his work as a journalist, he is going to have to fulfill his duties in different ways. For example, a special car may be required. Because of the limited use of his hand, he may need a modified computer keyboard or an assistant. An orientation and mobility specialist can serve as a client's advocate, negotiating with employers to prevent any cause for discrimination in the workplace. Specialists may also offer training and education programs to integrate or reintegrate the client into the workplace.

An orientation and mobility specialist also serves as a counselor. A client may need individual therapy or a support group. The family of the client may also need counseling on how to adjust to a parent's or child's disability.

Did You Know?

- More than 650 million people in the world have a disability; more than 54 million of this total reside in the United States.

- Arthritis is the leading cause of disability in the United States. The next most prevalent causes of disability (in descending order) are back or spine problems, heart trouble, lung or respiratory problems, mental or emotional problems, diabetes, deafness or other hearing problems, stiffness or deformity of limbs/extremities, blindness or vision problems, and stroke.

- Stroke is the leading cause of serious long-term disability in the United States. Each year, approximately 600,000 people in the United States experience a new or recurrent stroke.

Sources: American Association of People with Disabilities, Centers for Disease Control and Prevention

In addition to offering services that directly benefit the client (counseling, advocacy, education, and referral), some specialists may offer services that have indirect benefits for clients. These additional services include outreach, publicity, planning, and research. Because of a general lack of awareness of the social services available, orientation and mobility specialists may focus on ways to educate the public about the challenges facing those with disabilities. They may lead fund-raising efforts for research or programs aimed at assisting the disabled community.

REQUIREMENTS

High School

Because you will need a college degree and a well-rounded education, take your high school's program of college preparatory classes. These classes should include math and science courses as well as a foreign language. Strong communication skills are needed for this work, so to improve your skills in this area take four years of English. Speech and journalism classes are also beneficial. Courses in history, social studies, sociology, and psychology are also recommended.

Because a large part of the job is providing information about disability services, you should be comfortable using the Internet and various computer programs. Not only will you have to be able to work with computers yourself, you may be required to teach clients how to use them, too.

Postsecondary Training

The Association for Education and Rehabilitation of the Blind and Visually Impaired (commonly known as AER) provides a listing of approved orientation and mobility programs at the graduate, undergraduate, and certification-only levels. Programs include instruction in mobility techniques, where students simulate blindness or limited vision with blindfolds or other devices. Internships with disability agencies are also incorporated into the programs.

Other specialists prepare themselves for the career by studying social work. The Council on Social Work Education requires that five areas be covered in accredited bachelor's degree social work programs: human behavior and the social environment, social welfare policy and services, social work practice, research, and field practicum. Most programs require two years of liberal arts study, followed by two years of study in the social work major. Also, students must complete a field practicum of at least 400 hours.

Though some starting positions require only a bachelor's degree, most supervisory and administrative positions within social work require further education. Graduate programs are organized according to fields of practice (e.g., mental health care), problem areas (e.g., substance abuse), population groups (e.g., the elderly), and practice roles (e.g., practice with individuals, families, or communities). They are usually two-year programs with at least 900 hours of field practice. Doctoral degrees are also available for those interested in research, planning, or community outreach jobs.

Certification or Licensing

Only selected states require orientation and mobility specialists to be certified. The Academy for Certification of Vision Rehabilitation and Education Professionals offers certification for orientation and mobility specialists who meet certain educational and experience requirements. To be eligible to sit for the certification exam, individuals must first complete an AER-approved orientation and mobility program. Applicants who meet these certification requirements can use the designation, certified orientation and mobility specialist. Certification is also available in low vision therapy and vision rehabilitation therapy.

Other Requirements

For years, people with disabilities have faced discrimination. This discrimination is fueled by fear, by misunderstanding, and by the way people with disabilities are represented in popular culture. Orientation and mobility specialists must be able to honestly address their own perceptions of people with disabilities. Specialists must be sensitive to the client's situation and have a genuine interest in involving that person in the community and workplace.

Specialists also work frequently with the elderly, which requires understanding the aging experience. Workers must be patient and be good listeners to provide the elderly with the supportive network they need.

Communication skills are also very important. Much of the work as an orientation and mobility specialist involves talking and listening to clients, teaching, interviewing, and counseling. You will need to provide clear instructions to clients, their families, and their employers.

Because many of the problems facing those with disabilities stem from discrimination, many specialists work to educate the public about living with disabilities through research, reports, and fundraising. Being comfortable talking to a variety of people and in a variety of settings is an asset for these specialists.

EXPLORING

To learn more about this work, you can explore Web sites concerning disabilities and social work. A job in the school or public library helping people conduct research will put your information retrieval skills to good use. Working on the school newspaper will also help you develop your writing, researching, and interviewing skills, all important aspects of social work.

Part-time data entry jobs at a hospital or long-term care facility can familiarize you with medical terminology and the services available to people with disabilities. A part-time job in a retail pharmacy will involve you directly with people with disabilities and also the services that pay for the rental and purchase of wheelchairs, walkers, and canes. You can also gain experience by volunteering at any social service agency to get a sense of the work environment and responsibilities.

EMPLOYERS

Orientation and mobility specialists can find work with for-profit, nonprofit, and public programs. They may work in hospitals and community agencies such as transitional living services or with private agencies that focus on providing services specifically to those with disabilities.

An orientation and mobility specialist may also be self-employed, providing service on a contract basis to individuals or social service agencies.

STARTING OUT

To gain experience in social work, consider working with a social service agency specializing in information and referral. Rehabilitation centers, senior homes, schools, and summer camps for the blind, visually impaired, and disabled also offer many opportunities for experience. Because of limited funding, staffing may consist of only a few social work professionals, and the rest may be volunteers or assistants. Volunteer work may lead to full-time employment or simply introduce you to other social work professionals who can provide career guidance and letters of reference.

ADVANCEMENT

Orientation and mobility specialists may advance to become supervisors of assistants or executive directors of rehabilitation agencies. Another possible route for advancement is through teaching.

The more challenging and better-paying jobs tend to go to those with more years of practical experience and higher degrees. Further study, extensive experience, and good references will lead to advancement in the profession. Also, many social work programs offer continuing education workshops, courses, and seminars. These refresher courses help practicing specialists refine their skills and learn about new areas of practice, methods, and problems. These courses are intended to supplement previous education, not substitute for a bachelor's or master's degree. Continuing education can lead to job promotions and salary increases.

EARNINGS

The higher the degree held by specialists, the higher their earning potential. Those with a Ph.D. can take jobs in indirect service, research, and planning. Salaries also vary among regions; in general, social workers on the East and West Coasts earn higher salaries than those in the Midwest. During the first five years of practice, salaries increase faster than in later years.

Medical and public health social workers earned a median annual salary of $46,300 in 2009, according to the U.S. Department of Labor. The lowest paid 10 percent earned less than $28,600 and the highest paid 10 percent earned more than $71,190.

Specialists who work in school systems are generally paid on the same scale as teachers in the system. Those who work for private clients are usually paid by the hour or per session.

Orientation and mobility specialists usually receive benefits such as vacation days, sick leave, health and life insurance, and a savings and pension program. Self-employed specialists must provide their own benefits.

WORK ENVIRONMENT

Orientation and mobility specialists work part of the time in an office, analyzing and updating client files, interviewing clients over the phone, and talking with other service agencies. Depending on the size of the agency, office duties such as typing letters, filing, and answering phones may be performed by an aide or volunteer.

The rest of their time is spent outside the office, interacting directly with clients and others. Orientation and mobility specialists are involved directly with the people they serve and must carefully examine their clients' living conditions and family relations.

Advocacy involves work in a variety of different environments; it involves meetings with clients' employers, agency directors, and local legislators. Should the client press charges for discrimination, orientation and mobility specialists may be called upon to testify in court.

Both counseling and advocacy can be stressful aspects of the work, but helping to empower people with disabilities can be very rewarding.

OUTLOOK

According to the U.S. Census Bureau, more than 54 million people (approximately 19 percent of Americans) had a disability in 2008. In addition to continuing the fight against discrimination in the workplace and in general society, the disabled also need assistance in order to live productive lives.

Future funding is an important consideration for social service agencies. In many cases, the agencies providing information and referral must compete for funding with the very programs to which they refer people. This calls for good relationships between agencies and services. In order for agencies to receive adequate funding, social workers, including orientation and mobility specialists, must conduct research and provide reports to federal, state, and local governments showing proof of financial need. Their reports help to illustrate where funds should be allocated to best serve the disabled community.

According to the U.S. Department of Labor, the employment of social workers, including those who work with the visually and physically impaired, is expected to increase much faster than the average for all occupations through 2018. Specialists will continue to increase public awareness of the importance of aid for the disabled and visually impaired. Assistance services will continue to make their way into more public areas, such as libraries, workplaces, and other public facilities.

New computer technology will continue to cater to the special needs of the disabled. The development of specialized equipment and the expansion of Internet resources allow the disabled and visually impaired to access online resources for assistance. Orientation and mobility specialists will be needed to help those with disabilities use new technology to their best advantage.

FOR MORE INFORMATION

For information on certification, contact
Academy for Certification of Vision Rehabilitation and Education Professionals

3333 North Campbell Avenue, Suite 2
Tucson, AZ 85719-2361
Tel: 520-887-6816
http://www.acvrep.org

For resources and advocacy for the disabled community, contact
American Association of People with Disabilities
1629 K Street, NW, Suite 950
Washington, DC 20006-1675
Tel: 800-840-8844
http://www.aapd.com

For information on educational programs, contact
Association for Education and Rehabilitation of the Blind and Visually Impaired
1703 North Beauregard Street, Suite 440
Alexandria, VA 22311-1744
Tel: 877-492-2708
http://www.aerbvi.org

To read frequently asked questions about how to become a social worker, check out the following Web site:
Council on Social Work Education
1701 Duke Street, Suite 200
Alexandria, VA 22314-3415
Tel: 703-683-8080
E-mail: info@cswe.org
http://www.cswe.org

For information about careers, education, and job leads, contact
National Association of Social Workers
750 First Street, NE, Suite 700
Washington, DC 20002-4241
Tel: 202-408-8600
http://www.socialworkers.org

Physical Therapists

OVERVIEW

Physical therapists are health care specialists who restore mobility, alleviate pain and suffering, and work to prevent permanent disability for their patients. They test and measure the functions of the musculoskeletal, neurological, pulmonary, and cardiovascular systems and treat problems in these systems caused by illness, injury, or birth defect. Physical therapists provide preventive, restorative, and rehabilitative treatment for their patients. Approximately 185,500 physical therapists are licensed to practice in the United States.

HISTORY

The practice of physical therapy has developed as our knowledge of medicine and our understanding of the functions of the human body have grown. During the first part of the 20th century, there were tremendous strides in medical practice in general. The wartime experiences of medical teams who had to rehabilitate seriously injured soldiers contributed to the medical use and acceptance of physical therapy practices. The polio epidemic in the 1940s, which left many victims paralyzed, also led to the demand for improved physical therapy.

A professional association was organized in 1921, and physical therapy began to achieve professional stature. The American Physical Therapy Association (APTA) now serves a membership of more than 74,000 physical therapists, physical therapy assistants, and students. About 5,140 are members of its Section on Geriatrics.

A physical therapist works with an elderly man to help him to walk using parallel bars. *(John Birdsall, The Image Works)*

Today the use of physical therapy has expanded beyond hospitals, where it has been traditionally practiced. Physical therapists now are working in private practices, nursing homes, sports facilities, home health agencies, public and private schools, academic institutions, hospices, and in industrial physical therapy programs, a reflection of their versatility of skills and the public's need for comprehensive health care.

THE JOB

To initiate a program of physical therapy, the physical therapist consults the individual's medical history, examines the patient and identifies problems, confers with the physician or other health care professionals involved in the patient's care, establishes objectives and treatment goals that are consistent with the patient's needs, and determines the methods for accomplishing the objectives.

Treatment goals established by the physical therapist include preventing disability, relieving pain, and restoring function. In the presence of illness or injury, the ultimate goal is to assist the patient's physical recovery and reentry into the community, home, and work environment at the highest level of independence and self-sufficiency possible.

To aid and maintain recovery, the physical therapist also provides education to involve patients in their own care. The educational program may include exercises, posture reeducation, and relaxation practices. In many cases, the patient's family is involved in the educational program to provide emotional support or physical assistance as needed. These activities evolve into a continuum of self-care when the patient is discharged from the physical therapy program.

Physical therapists provide care for many types of patients of all ages. This includes working with burn victims to prevent abnormal scarring and loss of movement, with stroke victims to regain movement and independent living, with cancer patients to relieve discomfort, and with cardiac patients to improve endurance and achieve independence. Physical therapists also provide preventive exercise programs, postural improvement, and physical conditioning to individuals who perceive the need to promote their own health and well-being.

Physical therapists should have a creative approach to their work. No two patients respond the same way to exactly the same kind of treatment. The challenge is to find the right way to encourage the patient to make progress, to respond to treatment, to feel a sense of achievement, and to refuse to become discouraged if progress is slow.

Many physical therapists acquire specialized knowledge through clinical experience and educational preparation in specialty areas of practice, such as geriatric physical therapy, cardiopulmonary physical therapy, clinical electrophysiologic physical therapy, neurologic physical therapy, orthopedic physical therapy, pediatric physical therapy, and sports physical therapy. Physical therapists who specialize in geriatric care learn how to treat elderly patients with diseases and conditions such as Alzheimer's disease, amputations, arthritis, cancer, cardiac and pulmonary diseases, dementias, hip fractures, joint replacements, osteoporosis, Parkinson's disease, problems with balance and coordination, stroke, and urinary and fecal incontinence, among others.

REQUIREMENTS

High School

While you are in high school you can begin to prepare for this career by taking college preparatory classes. These should include biology, chemistry, physics, health, and mathematics. Because so much of this work involves direct contact with clients, you should improve your people skills as well as your communication skills by taking psychology, sociology, and English classes. Also, take computer science courses so that you are computer literate. Statistics, history, and a foreign language are also beneficial.

Postsecondary Training

Physical therapists attain their professional skills through extensive education that takes place both in the classroom and in clinical settings. You should attend a school accredited by the Commission on Accreditation in Physical Therapy Education (CAPTE) to receive the most thorough education. CAPTE now only accredits schools offering postbaccalaureate degrees (master's and doctorate degrees), and you will need one of these degrees to practice physical therapy. Previously, CAPTE had accredited bachelor's degree programs; however, this change was made to give students an appropriate amount of time to study liberal arts as well as a physical therapy curriculum. Course work should include classes in the humanities as well as those geared for the profession, such as anatomy, human growth and development, and therapeutic procedures. Clinical experience is done as supervised fieldwork in such settings as hospitals, home care agencies, and nursing homes. According to the APTA, there are 12 accredited programs offering master's degrees and 200 offering doctorates in physical therapy.

Employment Settings for Physical Therapists, 2007

Private outpatient or group practice: 41.5 percent

Health system or hospital-based outpatient facility or clinic: 14.5 percent

Acute care hospital: 13.1 percent

Patient's home/home care: 7.9 percent

All other work settings: 23 percent

Source: American Physical Therapy Association

After graduation, many physical therapists who plan to specialize in geriatrics participate in residencies in which they gain specialized experience working with the elderly. Visit http://www.geriatricspt.org/geriatric-residencies-fellowships.cfm for more information about residency programs.

Certification or Licensing

Specialist certification of physical therapists, while not a requirement for employment, is a desirable advanced credential. The American Board of Physical Therapy Specialties, an appointed group of the American Physical Therapy Association, certifies physical therapists who demonstrate specialized knowledge and advanced clinical proficiency in a specialty area of physical therapy practice and who pass a certifying examination. The areas of specialization are cardiovascular and pulmonary, clinical electrophysiologic, neurologic, orthopaedics, pediatrics, geriatrics, sports, and women's health. The board also offers the certified exercise expert for aging adults designation.

Upon graduating from an accredited physical therapy educational program, all physical therapists must successfully complete a national licensing examination. Other licensing requirements vary by state. You will need to check with the licensing board of the state in which you hope to work for specific information.

Other Requirements

Successful physical therapists enjoy working with people and helping others to feel better, both physically and emotionally. They need creativity and patience to determine a treatment plan for each client and to help them achieve treatment goals. Physical therapists must also be committed to lifelong learning because new developments in technology and medicine mean that therapists must continually update their knowledge. It is also a plus to have a positive attitude and an outgoing personality.

EXPLORING

Your first step in exploring this field could be to talk with a physical therapist in your community about the work. Your school counselor should be able to help you arrange for such an information interview. Hands-on experience is important to get because schools that you apply to will take this into consideration. This experience will also help you decide how well you like working with people who are sometimes in pain or confused. One possibility is to volunteer at a physical therapy program. If such an opening is not available, try volunteering at a local hospital, nursing home, or other care facility to gain experience working in these settings. You can also look for volunteer opportunities or summer jobs at camps for the disabled. Paid part-time positions may also be available as a hospital orderly or aide to a physical therapist.

EMPLOYERS

Approximately 185,500 physical therapists are employed in the United States. Hospitals and offices of physical therapists employ the majority of physical therapists. According to the U.S. Department of Labor, the rest work in settings such as offices of physicians, private physical therapy offices, community health centers, sports facilities, nursing care facilities, home health care, and schools. Physical therapists may be involved in research or teach at colleges and universities. Veterans Administration hospitals and other government agencies also hire physical therapists. Some physical therapists are self-employed.

STARTING OUT

Physical therapy graduates may obtain jobs through their college career services offices or by answering ads in any of a variety of professional journals. They can apply in person or send letters and resumes to hospitals, nursing homes, medical centers, rehabilitation facilities, and other places that hire physical therapists. Some find jobs through the American Physical Therapy Association, which offers a job bank at its Web site, http://www.apta.org.

ADVANCEMENT

In a hospital or other health care facility, one may rise from being a staff physical therapist to being the chief physical therapist and then director of the department. Administrative responsibilities are usually given to those physical therapists who have had several years of experience plus the personal qualities that prepare them for undertaking this kind of assignment.

After serving in a hospital or other institution for several years, some physical therapists open up their own practices or go into a group practice, with both often paying higher salaries.

EARNINGS

Salaries for physical therapists depend on experience and type of employer. Physical therapists earned an annual average salary of $74,480 in 2009, according to the U.S. Department of Labor (DOL). Fifty percent averaged between $62,270 and $87,940; the top paid 10 percent earned $105,900 or more a year. Those just starting out in the field earned less than $52,170. The DOL reports that physical therapists earned the following salaries by employer: home health care services, $83,500; individual and family services, $80,390; nursing care facilities, $78,990; offices of physicians, $77,120; offices of other health practitioners, $75,760; and general medical and surgical hospitals, $75,030.

Salaried physical therapists also enjoy fringe benefits such as paid vacation, 401 (k) savings plans, and medical and dental insurance. Self-employed physical therapists must provide their own benefits.

WORK ENVIRONMENT

The typical physical therapist works approximately 40 hours each week, including evenings and weekends. Patient sessions may be brief or may last an hour or more. Usually, treatment is on an individual basis, but occasionally therapy may be given in groups when the patients' problems are similar.

OUTLOOK

Employment for physical therapists is expected to grow much faster than the average for all occupations through 2018, according to the DOL. One reason for this strong growth is the fact that the median age of the American population is rising, and this older demographic group develops a higher number of medical conditions that cause physical pain and disability. The DOL reports that employment should be especially strong in acute hospital, orthopedic, and rehabilitation settings, where elderly patients are most often treated. Also, advances in medical technology save more people, who then require physical therapy. For example, as more trauma victims and newborns with birth defects survive, the need for physical therapists will rise. Another reason is the public's growing interest in physical fitness, which has resulted in an increasing number of athletic injuries requiring physical therapy. In industry and fitness centers, a growing interest in pain and injury prevention also has created new opportunities for physical therapists.

Employment prospects for physical therapists should continue to be good into the next decade. If enrollment in accredited physical therapy programs remains at the current level, there will be more openings for physical therapists than qualified individuals to fill them.

FOR MORE INFORMATION

For information on careers and certification and a directory of accredited schools, contact
American Physical Therapy Association
1111 North Fairfax Street
Alexandria, VA 22314-1488
Tel: 800-999-2782, ext. 2782
http://www.apta.org
http://www.geriatricspt.org

For information on accredited programs, contact
Commission on Accreditation in Physical Therapy Education
http://www.apta.org/CAPTE

Recreational Therapists

QUICK FACTS

School Subjects
Biology
Psychology

Personal Skills
Helping/teaching
Technical/scientific

Work Environment
Indoors and outdoors
Primarily one location

Minimum Education Level
Bachelor's degree

Salary Range
$24,510 to $39,440 to
$62,170+

Certification or Licensing
Required by certain states

Outlook
Faster than the average

DOT
076

GOE
14.06.01

NOC
3144

O*NET-SOC
29-1125.00

OVERVIEW

Recreational therapists, also known as *therapeutic recreation specialists*, plan, organize, direct, and monitor medically approved recreation programs for patients in hospitals, clinics, and various community settings. These therapists use recreational activities to assist patients with mental, physical, or emotional disabilities to achieve the maximum possible functional independence. Recreational therapists hold approximately 23,300 jobs in the United States.

HISTORY

The field of therapy has expanded in the past few decades to include recreational therapy as a form of medical treatment. Its use grew out of the realization that soldiers suffering from battle fatigue, shock, and emotional trauma respond positively to organized recreation and activity programs.

As a result, therapy for people in nursing homes, hospitals, mental institutions, and adult care facilities is no longer limited to physical therapy. Experiments have shown that recovery is aided by recreational activities such as sports, music, art, gardening, dance, drama, field trips, and other pastimes. Elderly people are more healthy and alert when their days are filled with activities, field trips, and social get-togethers. People with disabilities can gain greater self-confidence and awareness of their own abilities when they get involved with sports, crafts, and other activities. People recovering from drug or alcohol addiction can reaffirm their self-worth through directed hobbies, clubs, and sports. The recreational therapist is a health professional who organizes these types of activities and helps patients take an active role in their own recovery.

THE JOB

Recreational therapists work with people who are mentally, physically, or emotionally disabled. They are professionals who employ leisure activities as a form of treatment, much as other health practitioners use surgery, drugs, nutrition, exercise, or psychotherapy. Recreational therapists strive to minimize patients' symptoms, restore function, and improve their physical, mental, and emotional well-being. Enhancing the patient's ability to take part in everyday life is the primary goal of recreational therapy; interesting and rewarding activities are the means for working toward that goal.

Recreational therapists work in a number of different settings, including nursing homes, adult day care programs, mental hospitals, psychiatric day hospitals, community mental health centers, residential facilities for the mentally disabled, school systems, and prisons. They can work as individual staff members, as independent consultants, or as part of a larger therapeutic team. They may get personally involved with patients or direct the work of assistants and support staff.

The recreational therapist first confers with the doctors, psychiatrists, social workers, physical therapists, and other professionals on staff to coordinate their efforts in treatment. The recreational therapist needs to understand the nature of the patient's ailment, current physical and mental capacities, emotional state, and prospects for recovery. The patient's family and friends are also consulted to find out the patient's interests and hobbies. With this information, the recreational therapist then plans an agenda of activities for that person.

To enrich the lives of people in hospitals and other institutions, recreational therapists use imagination and skill in organizing beneficial activities. Sports, games, arts and crafts, movie screenings, field trips, hobby clubs, and dramatics are only a few examples of activities that can enrich the lives of patients. Some therapists specialize in certain areas. *Dance/movement therapists* plan and conduct dance and body movement exercises to improve patients' physical and mental well-being. *Art therapists* work with patients in various art methods, such as drawing, painting, and ceramics, as part of their therapeutic and recovery programs. Therapists may also work with pets and other animals, such as horses. *Music therapists* design programs for patients that can involve solo or group singing, playing in bands, rhythmic and other creative activities, listening to music, or attending concerts. Even flowers and gardening can prove beneficial to patients, as is proved by the work of *horticultural therapists*. When the treatment team feels that regular employment would help certain patients, the *industrial therapist* arranges a productive job for the patient in an actual work environment, one that will have the greatest therapeutic value based on the patient's needs and abilities. *Orientation therapists* for the blind work with people who have recently lost their sight, helping them to readjust to daily living and independence through training and exercise. All of these professional therapists plan their programs to meet the needs and capabilities of patients. They also carefully monitor and record each patient's progress and report it to the other members of the medical team.

As part of their jobs, recreational therapists need to understand their patients and set goals for their progress accordingly. A patient having trouble socializing, for example, may have an interest in playing chess but be overwhelmed by the prospect of actually playing, since that involves interaction with another person. A therapist would proceed slowly, first letting the patient observe a number of games and then assigning a therapeutic assistant to serve as a chess partner for weeks or even months, as long as it takes for the patient to gain enough confidence to seek out other patients for chess partners. The therapist makes a note of the patient's response, modifies the therapy program accordingly, and lets other professionals know of the results. If a patient responds more enthusiastically to the program, works more cooperatively with others, or becomes more disruptive, the therapist must note these reactions and periodically reevaluate the patient's activity program.

Responsibilities and elements of the job can vary, depending on the setting in which the recreational therapist works. In nursing homes, the therapist often groups residents according to common or shared interests and ability levels and then plans field trips, parties, entertainment, and other group activities. The therapist documents residents' responses to the activities and continually searches for ways of heightening residents' enjoyment of recreational and leisure activities, not just in the facility but in the surrounding community as well. Because nursing home residents are likely to remain in the facility for months or even years, the activities program makes a big difference in the quality of their lives. Without the stimulation of interesting events to look forward to and participate in, the daily routine of a nursing home can become monotonous and depress-

Books to Read

Austin, David R. *Therapeutic Recreation: Processes and Techniques*. 6th ed. Urbana, Ill.: Sagamore Publishing, 2009.

Carter, Marcia Jean, Gary M. Robb, and Glen E. Van Andel. *Therapeutic Recreation: A Practical Approach*. 3d ed. Long Grove, Ill.: Waveland Press, 2003.

Robertson, Terry, and Terry Long. *Foundations of Therapeutic Recreation*. Champaign, Ill.: Human Kinetics Publishers, 2008.

Stumbo, Norma J., and Carol Ann Peterson. *Therapeutic Recreation Program Design: Principles and Procedures*. 5th ed. San Francisco, Calif.: Benjamin Cummings Publishing Company, 2008.

Wilhite, Barbara, and Jean Keller. *Therapeutic Recreation: Cases and Exercises*. 2d ed. State College, Pa.: Venture Publishing, 2001.

ing, and some residents are apt to deteriorate both mentally and physically. In some nursing homes, recreational therapists direct the activities program. In others, activities coordinators plan and carry out the program under the part-time supervision of a consultant who is either a recreational or occupational therapist.

The therapist in a community center might work in a day care program for the elderly or in a program for mentally disabled adults operated by a county recreation department. No matter what the disability, recreational therapists in community settings face the added logistical challenge of arranging transportation and escort services, if necessary, for prospective participants. Coordinating transportation is less of a problem in hospitals and nursing homes, where the patients all live under one roof. Developing therapeutic recreation programs in community settings requires a large measure of organizational ability, flexibility, and ingenuity.

REQUIREMENTS

High School

You can prepare for a career as a recreational therapist by taking your high school's college preparatory program. Naturally, this should include science classes, such as biology and chemistry, as well as mathematics and history classes. You can begin to gain an understanding of human behavior by taking psychology and sociology classes. For exposure to a variety of recreation specialties, take physical education, art, music, and drama classes. Verbal and written communication skills are essential for this work, so take English and speech classes. This job will require you to write reports, so computer science skills are also essential.

Postsecondary Training

More than 100 recreational therapy programs, which offer degrees ranging from the associate to the doctoral level, are currently available in the United States. While associate degrees in recreational therapy exist, such a degree will allow you only to work at the paraprofessional level. To be eligible for an entry-level professional position as a recreational therapist, you will need a bachelor's degree. Acceptable majors are recreational therapy, therapeutic recreation, and recreation with a concentration in therapeutic recreation. A typical four-year bachelor's degree program includes courses in both natural science (such as biology, behavioral science, and human anatomy) and social science (such as psychology and sociology). Courses more specific to the profession include programming for special populations (such as the elderly); rehabilitative techniques including self-help skills, mobility, signing for the deaf, and orientation for the blind; medical equipment; current treatment approaches; legal issues; and professional ethics. In addition, you will need to complete a supervised internship or field placement lasting a minimum of 480 hours.

Continuing education is increasingly becoming a requirement for professionals in this field. Many therapists attend conferences and seminars and take additional university courses. A number of professional organizations (for example, the National Therapeutic Recreation Society and the American Therapeutic Recreation Association) offer continuing education opportunities. Those with degrees in related fields can enter the profession by earning master's degrees in therapeutic recreation or recreational therapy. Advanced degrees are recommended for those seeking advancement to supervisory, administrative, and teaching positions. These requirements will become more strict as more professionals enter the field.

Certification or Licensing

A number of states regulate the profession of therapeutic recreation. Licensing is required in some states; professional certification (or eligibility for certification) is required in others; titling is regulated in some states and at some facilities. In other states, many hospitals and other employers require recreational therapists to be certified. Certification is recommended for recreational therapists as a way to show professional accomplishment. It is available through the National Council for Therapeutic Recreation Certification. To receive certification you must meet eligibility requirements, including education and experience, as well as pass an exam. You are then given the title of certified therapeutic recreation specialist. Because of the variety of certification and licensing requirements, you must check with both your state and your employer for specific information on your situation. Most clinical settings require therapists to be certified.

Other Requirements

To be a successful recreational therapist, you must enjoy and be enthusiastic about the activities in which you involve your clients. You will also need patience and a positive attitude. Since this is people-oriented work, therapists must be able to relate to many different people in a variety of settings. They must be able to deal assertively and politely with other health care workers, such as doctors and nurses, as well as with the clients themselves and their families. In addition, successful therapists must be creative and have strong communication skills in order to develop and explain activities to patients.

EXPLORING

If you are interested in recreational therapy, you can find part-time or summer work as a sports coach or referee, park supervisor, or camp counselor. Volunteer work in a nursing home, hospital, or care facility for disabled adults is also a good way to learn about the daily realities of institutional living. These types of facilities are always looking for volunteers to work with and visit patients. Working with people with physical, mental, or emotional disabilities can be stressful, and volunteer work is a good way for you to test whether you can handle this kind of stress.

EMPLOYERS

Recreational therapists hold approximately 23,300 jobs, according to the U.S. Department of Labor. About 24 percent of these jobs are in nursing care facilities. Other employers include residential care facilities, hospitals, adult day care centers, substance abuse centers, and state and local government agencies. Some therapists are self-employed. Employment opportunities also exist in long-term rehabilitation, home health care, correctional facilities, psychiatric facilities, and transitional programs.

STARTING OUT

There are many methods for finding out about available jobs in recreational therapy. A good place to start is the job notices and want ads printed in the local newspapers, bulletins from state park and recreation societies, and publications of the professional associations previously mentioned. State employment agencies and human service departments will know of job openings in state hospitals. College career services offices might also be able to put new recreational therapy graduates in touch with prospective employers. Internship programs are sometimes available, offering good opportunities to find potential full-time jobs.

Recent graduates should also make appointments to meet potential employers personally. Most colleges and universities offer career counseling services. Most employers will make themselves available to discuss their programs and the possibility of hiring extra staff. They may also guide new graduates to other institutions currently hiring therapists. Joining professional associations, both state and national, and attending conferences are good ways to meet potential employers and colleagues.

ADVANCEMENT

Newly graduated recreational therapists generally begin as *staff therapists*. Advancement is chiefly to supervisory or administrative positions, usually after some years of experience and continuing education. Some therapists teach, conduct research, or do consulting work on a contract basis; a graduate degree is essential for moving into these areas.

Many therapists continue their education but prefer to continue working with patients. For variety, they may choose to work with new groups of people or get a job in a new setting, such as moving from a facility for the disabled to a retirement home. Some may also move to a related field, such as special education, or sales positions involving products and services related to recreational therapy.

EARNINGS

Salaries of recreational therapists vary according to educational background, experience, certification, and region of the country. Recreational therapists had median earnings of $39,440 in 2009, according to the U.S. Department of Labor. The lowest paid 10 percent earned less than $24,510 a year, while the highest paid 10 percent earned more than $62,170 annually. Employment setting is also an important factor in determining salary. Recreational therapists employed by nursing care facilities earned mean incomes of $36,210, while those employed by general medical and surgical hospitals earned $44,840. Those in management positions command higher salaries. Salaries for supervisors range from $50,000 to $75,000 or more annually; and some consultants and educators reported even higher earnings.

Therapists employed at hospitals, clinics, and other facilities generally enjoy a full benefits package, including health insurance and vacation, holiday, and sick pay. Consultants and self-employed therapists must provide their own benefits.

WORK ENVIRONMENT

Working conditions vary, but recreational therapists generally work in a ward, a specially equipped activity room, or at a nursing home. In a community setting, recreational therapists may interview subjects and plan activities in an office, but they might work in a gymnasium, swimming pool, playground, or outdoors on a nature walk when leading activities. Therapists may also work on horse ranches, farms, and other outdoor facilities catering to people with disabilities.

The job may be physically tiring because therapists are often on their feet all day and may have to lift and carry equipment. Recreational therapists generally work a standard 40-hour week, although weekend and evening hours may be required. Supervisors may have to work overtime, depending on their workload.

OUTLOOK

The U.S. Department of Labor predicts that employment for recreational therapists will grow faster than the average for all occupations through 2018. Employment in nursing homes will grow slightly faster than in other areas. Fast employment growth is expected in assisted living, outpatient physical and psychiatric rehabilitation, and services for people with disabilities. Increased life expectancies for the elderly and for people with developmental disabilities such as Down Syndrome will create opportunities for recreational therapists. The incidence of alcohol and drug dependency problems is also growing, creating a demand for qualified therapists to work in short-term alcohol and drug abuse clinics.

Most openings for recreational therapists will be in health care and assisted living facilities because of the increasing numbers and greater longevity of the elderly. There is also greater public pressure to regulate and improve the quality of life in retirement centers, which may mean more jobs and increased scrutiny of recreational therapists.

Growth in hospital jobs is not expected to be great. Many of the new jobs created will be in hospital-based adult day care programs or in units offering short-term mental health services. Because of economic and social factors, little growth is expected in public mental hospitals. Many of the programs and services formerly offered there are being shifted to community residential facilities for the disabled. Community programs for special populations are expected to expand significantly.

FOR MORE INFORMATION

For career information and resources, contact
American Association for Physical Activity and Recreation
1900 Association Drive
Reston, VA 20191-1598
Tel: 703-476-3430
E-mail: aapar@aahperd.org
http://www.aahperd.org/aapar

For career information, a list of colleges and universities that offer training, and job listings, contact
American Therapeutic Recreation Association
629 North Main Street
Hattiesburg, MS 39401-3429
Tel: 601-450-2872
http://www.atra-online.com

For information on certification, contact
National Council for Therapeutic Recreation Certification
7 Elmwood Drive
New City, NY 10956-5136
Tel: 845-639-1439
E-mail: nctrc@nctrc.org
http://www.nctrc.org

For career information, contact
National Therapeutic Recreation Society
22377 Belmont Ridge Road
Ashburn, VA 20148-4501
Tel: 800-626-6772
http://www.nrpa.org/ntrs

Visit this Web site to find out about jobs, activities, schools, and other information related to the field.

Rehabilitation Counselors

Therapeutic Recreation Directory
http://www.recreationtherapy.com

OVERVIEW

Rehabilitation counselors provide counseling and guidance services to people with disabilities to help them resolve life problems and to train for and locate work that is suitable to their physical and mental abilities, interests, and aptitudes. They also help them to live independently. There are approximately 129,500 rehabilitation counselors working in the United States.

HISTORY

Today it is generally accepted that people with disabilities can and should have the opportunity to become as fully independent as possible in all aspects of life, from school to work and social activities. In response to the needs of disabled war veterans, Congress passed the first Vocational Rehabilitation Act in 1920. The act set in place the Vocational Rehabilitation Program, a federal-state program that provides for the delivery of rehabilitation services, including counseling, to eligible people with disabilities.

The profession of rehabilitation counseling has its roots in the Rehabilitation Act, which allowed for funds to train personnel. What was at first a job title developed into a fully recognized profession as it became evident that the delivery of effective rehabilitation services required highly trained specialists. Early efforts for providing rehabilitation counseling and other services

QUICK FACTS

School Subjects
Psychology
Sociology

Personal Skills
Helping/teaching
Technical/scientific

Work Environment
Primarily indoors
Primarily one location

Minimum Education Level
Master's degree

Salary Range
$20,440 to $31,210 to
$55,580+

Certification or Licensing
Required for certain
positions (certification)
Required by certain stares
(licensing)

Outlook
Faster than the average

DOT
045

GOE
12.02.02

NOC
4153

O*NET-SOC
21-1015.00

were often directed especially toward the nation's veterans. In 1930, the Veterans Administration was created to supply support services to veterans and their families, and in 1989, the U.S. Department of Veterans Affairs was created as the 14th cabinet department in the U.S. government.

The passage of the Americans with Disabilities Act in 1990 recognized the rights and needs of people with disabilities and developed federal regulations and guidelines aimed at eliminating discrimination and other barriers preventing people with disabilities from participating fully in school, workplace, and public life. Many state and federal programs have since been created to aid people with disabilities.

THE JOB

Rehabilitation counselors work with people with disabilities to identify barriers to medical, psychological, personal, social, and vocational functioning and to develop a plan of action to remove or reduce those barriers.

Clients are referred to rehabilitation programs from many sources. Sometimes they seek help on their own initiative; sometimes their families bring them in. They may be referred by a physician, hospital, or social worker, or they may be sent by employment agencies, schools, or accident commissions. A former employer may seek help for the individual.

The counselor's first step is to determine the nature and extent of the disability and evaluate how that disability interferes with work and other life functions. This determination is made from medical and psychological reports as well as from family history, educational background, work experience, and other evaluative information.

The next step is to determine a vocational direction and plan of services to overcome the handicaps to employment or independent living.

The rehabilitation counselor coordinates a comprehensive evaluation of a client's physical functioning abilities and vocational interests, aptitudes, and skills. This information is used to develop vocational or independent-living goals for the client and the services necessary to reach those goals. Services that the rehabilitation counselor may coordinate or provide include physical and mental restoration, academic or vocational training, vocational counseling, job analysis, job modification or reasonable accommodation, and job placement. Limited financial assistance in the form of maintenance or transportation assistance may also be provided.

The counselor's relationship with the client may be as brief as a week or as long as several years, depending on the nature of the problem and the needs of the client.

REQUIREMENTS

High School

To prepare for a career in rehabilitation counseling, take your high school's college preparatory curriculum. These classes should include several years of mathematics and science, such as biology and chemistry. To begin to gain an understanding of people and societies, take history, psychology, and sociology classes. English classes are important to take because you will need excellent communication skills for this work. Some of your professional responsibilities will include documenting your work and doing research to provide your clients with helpful information; to do these things you will undoubtedly be working with computers. Therefore, you should take computer science classes so that you are skilled in using them. In addition, you may want to consider taking speech and a foreign language, both of which will enhance your communication skills.

Postsecondary Training

Although some positions are available for people with a bachelor's degree in rehabilitation counseling, these positions are usually as aides and offer limited advancement opportunities. Most employers require the rehabilitation counselors working for them to hold master's degrees. Before receiving your master's, you will need to complete a bachelor's degree with a major in behavioral sciences, social sciences, or a related field. Another option is to complete an undergraduate degree in rehabilitation counseling. No matter which undergraduate program you decide on, you should concentrate on courses in sociology, psychology, physiology, history, and statistics as well as courses in English and communications. Several universities now offer courses in various aspects of physical therapy and special education training. Courses in sign language, speech therapy, and a foreign language are also beneficial.

Both the Council for Accreditation of Counseling and Related Educational Programs and the Council on Rehabilitation Education accredit graduate counseling programs. A typical master's program in rehabilitation counseling usually lasts two years. Studies include courses in medical aspects of disability, psychosocial aspects of disability, testing techniques, statistics, personality theory, personality development, abnormal psychology, techniques of counseling, occupational information, and vocational training and job placement. A supervised internship is also an important aspect of a program.

Certification or Licensing

The regulation of counselors is required in 49 states and the District of Columbia. This regulation may be in the form of credentialing, registry, certification, or licensure. Regulations, however, vary by state and sometimes by employer. For example, an employer may require certification even if the state does not. You will need to check with your state's licensing board as well as your employer for specific information about your circumstances.

Across the country, many employers now require their rehabilitation counselors to be certified by the Commission on Rehabilitation Counselor Certification (CRCC). The purpose of certification is to provide assurance that professionals engaged in rehabilitation counseling meet set standards and maintain those standards through continuing education. To become certified, counselors must pass an extensive multiple-choice examination to demonstrate their knowledge of rehabilitation counseling. The CRCC requires the master's degree as the minimum educational level for certification. Applicants who meet these certification requirements receive the designation of certified rehabilitation counselor.

Most state government rehabilitation agencies require future counselors to meet state civil service and merit system regulations. The applicant must take a competitive written examination and may also be interviewed and evaluated by a special board.

Other Requirements

The most important personal attribute required for rehabilitation counseling is the ability to get along well with other people. Rehabilitation counselors work with many different kinds of clients and must be able to see situations and problems from their client's point of view. They must be both patient and persistent. Rehabilitation may be a slow process with many delays and setbacks. The counselor must maintain a calm, positive manner even when no progress is made.

EXPLORING

To explore a career in which you work with people with disabilities, you should look for opportunities to volunteer or work in this field. One possibility is to be a counselor at a children's camp for disabled youngsters. You can also volunteer with a local vocational rehabilitation agency or a facility such as the Easter Seal Society or Goodwill. Other possibilities include reading for the blind or leading a hobby or craft class at an adult day care center. And don't forget volunteer opportunities at a local hospital or nursing home. Even if your only responsibility is to escort people to the X-ray department or talk to patients to cheer them up, you will gain valuable experience interacting with people who are facing challenging situations.

EMPLOYERS

Approximately 129,500 rehabilitation counselors are employed in the United States. Counselors work in a variety of settings. About three-quarters of rehabilitation counselors work for state agencies; some also work for local and federal agencies. Employment opportunities are available in rehabilitation centers, mental health agencies, developmental disability agencies, sheltered workshops, training institutions, and special schools. Other rehabilitation counselors teach at colleges and universities.

STARTING OUT

School career services offices are the best places for the new graduate to begin the career search. In addition, the National Rehabilitation Counseling Association and the American Rehabilitation Counseling Association (a division of the American Counseling Association) are sources for employment information. The new counselor may also apply directly to agencies for available positions. State and local vocational rehabilitation agencies employ more than 27,900 rehabilitation counselors. The U.S. Department of Veterans Affairs employs counselors to assist with the rehabilitation of disabled veterans. Many rehabilitation counselors are employed by private for-profit or nonprofit rehabilitation programs and facilities. Others are employed in industry, schools, hospitals, and other settings, while others are self-employed.

ADVANCEMENT

The rehabilitation counselor usually receives regular salary increases after gaining experience in the job. He or she may move from relatively easy cases to increasingly challenging ones. Counselors may advance into such positions as administrator or supervisor after several years of counseling experience. It is also possible to find related counseling and teaching positions, which may represent an advancement in other fields.

EARNINGS

Salaries for rehabilitation counselors vary widely according to state, community, employer, and the counselor's experience. The U.S. Department of Labor reports that median annual earnings of rehabilitation counselors in 2009 were $31,210. Salaries ranged from less than $20,440 to more than $55,580.

Rehabilitation counselors employed by the federal government generally start at the GS-9 or GS-11 level. In 2009, basic GS-9 salary was $40,949. Those with master's degrees generally began at the GS-11 level, with a salary of $49,544 in 2009. Salaries for federal government workers vary according to the region of the country in which they work. Those working in areas with a higher cost of living receive additional locality pay.

Counselors employed by government and private agencies and institutions generally receive health insurance, pension plans, and other benefits, including vacation, sick, and holiday pay. Self-employed counselors must provide their own benefits.

WORK ENVIRONMENT

Rehabilitation counselors work approximately 40 hours each week and do not usually have to work during evenings or weekends. They work both in the office and in the field. Depending on the type of training required, lab space and workout or therapy rooms may be available. Rehabilitation counselors must usually keep detailed accounts of their progress with clients and write reports. They may spend many hours traveling to visit employed clients, prospective employers, trainees, or training programs.

OUTLOOK

The passage of the Americans with Disabilities Act of 1990 increased the demand for rehabilitation counselors. As more local, state, and federal programs are initiated that are designed to assist people with disabilities and as private institutions and companies seek to comply with this new legislation, job prospects are promising. Budget pressures may serve to limit the number of new rehabilitation counselors to be hired by government agencies; however, the overall outlook remains excellent.

The U.S. Department of Labor predicts that employment for rehabilitation counselors will grow faster than average for all occupations through 2018. Some of this growth can be attributed to the advances in medical technology that are saving more lives and allowing people to live longer. Legislation requiring that people with disabilities receive equal treatment under the law will also create increasing opportunities for rehabilitation counselors.

FOR MORE INFORMATION

For general information on careers in rehabilitation counseling, contact
American Rehabilitation Counseling Association
5999 Stevenson Avenue
Alexandria, VA 22304-3300
http://www.arcaweb.org

For information on certification, contact
Commission on Rehabilitation Counselor Certification
1699 East Woodfield Road, Suite 300
Schaumburg, IL 60173-4957
Tel: 847-944-1325
E-mail: info@crccertification.com
http://www.crccertification.com

For listings of CORE-approved programs as well as other information, contact
Council on Rehabilitation Education (CORE)
1699 East Woodfield Road, Suite 300
Schaumburg, IL 60173-4957
Tel: 847-944-1345
http://www.core-rehab.org

For information on a variety of rehabilitation resources, contact
National Clearinghouse of Rehabilitation Training Materials
Utah State University
6524 Old Main Hill
Logan, UT 84322-6524
Tel: 866-821-5355
E-mail: ncrtm@usu.edu
http://ncrtm.org

To learn about government legislation, visit the association's Web site.

National Rehabilitation Association
633 South Washington Street
Alexandria, VA 22314-4109
Tel: 703-836-0850
E-mail: info@nationalrehab.org
http://www.nationalrehab.org

The NRCA is a division of the National Rehabilitation Association. For news on legislation, employment, and other information, contact

settings, and their responsibilities vary based on the places of work. In general, however, senior care pharmacists' duties involve consulting with nursing facilities or other long-term care facilities (such as assisted living facilities, hospices, and home-based care programs) about the condition and care of their patients. These pharmacists do on-site visits to meet with their patients, discuss any problems they may be having as well as to discuss a treatment plan, and meet with the other health care professionals who are part of a team caring for the patient.

An important aspect of the senior care pharmacist's work is to conduct regular drug regimen reviews as required by law. For these reviews, senior care pharmacists gather and review information on a patient's medical history, diagnosis, test results, and treatments. In general, they go over any information related to the person's health, including his or her diet. The pharmacist also meets with the patient's doctors, nurses, and any other health professional involved in the patient's care to review treatment plans and goals. Senior care pharmacists then go over the medications prescribed for the patient, checking to make sure the patients are receiving the right medicines, in the right doses, and at the right times. If the senior care pharmacist discovers a problem with a medication being given, he or she figures out how to correct the situation.

Some of the unique knowledge senior care pharmacists have includes knowing how a medicine will affect an older person's body, knowing how different medicines will react together in clients who take more than one prescription, knowing if a medication will make an elderly person's existing conditions worse, and, just as important, knowing the life circumstances of the patient. That is, the pharmacist should know the answer to questions such as: Is someone available to give the medication to the patient on a regular basis? Or, if the patient is in an assisted living facility, will he or she remember to take the medicine? Is the patient skipping doses to make a prescription last longer? Can the patient read the instruction label? Does the patient still need the medicine, or has he or she recovered from the illness the medicine was treating? Senior care pharmacists need to be aware of all such factors in order to find appropriate solutions to any problems that may arise.

In addition to having a close relationship with other health care professionals, senior care pharmacists must have close relationships with their clients, treating each as an individual. Because an older person's body processes medication differently than a younger person's, senior care pharmacists must be able to customize medications for their patients so that they achieve the desired results. A pharmacist may suggest, for example, taking two doses of a medicine at different times during the day instead of one large dose that is more difficult for an older person's body to absorb. Many older people regularly take more than one type of drug for a variety of problems. And senior care pharmacists must know when 70-year-old Mr. Jones, for example, comes in with a prescription for a new arthritis medicine if this medicine will interfere with the effectiveness of the blood pressure medicine he is already taking. If the potential for negative drug interaction exists, the pharmacist will consult with the doctor and suggest a more appropriate treatment.

Senior care pharmacists must also understand a patient's overall health condition. Many older people, for example, have a poor sense of balance, limited vision, or are forgetful. Senior care pharmacists must know if a patient experiences any such problems so that they do not give a medicine that will make the situation worse. For example, if 82-year-old Ms. Braun (who has osteoporosis and is unsteady walking) has a prescription for a medicine that has the side effect of causing dizziness, the pharmacist should realize this might aggravate her balance problem and lead to a fall that could cause broken bones. In such a case, the senior care pharmacist will advise Ms. Braun's doctor about the problem and recommend a different medication.

Senior care pharmacists also keep detailed records of drugs dispensed to each client. This is extremely important because older people often see more than one doctor for a number of different conditions. The senior care pharmacist may be the only person keeping track of various medicines prescribed by several doctors for one patient. In these cases, the senior care pharmacist is the health care professional who is in the best position to spot a potential adverse drug interaction and recommend a prescription change.

Another responsibility of senior care pharmacists is to answer questions about medications and provide training to other health care workers on how to administer these medications. A senior care pharmacist may spend part of a day or a whole day, for example, giving nurses at a nursing home instruction on how to figure out the proper dose of an antibiotic that will be given through an IV. Naturally, senior care pharmacists also spend time in the pharmacy, where their activities include reviewing and documenting incoming prescriptions, supervising pharmacy technicians, checking filled prescriptions for their correctness, and answering questions about medications.

Like all pharmacists, senior care pharmacists must be diligent in maintaining clean and ordered work areas. They must be exceedingly accurate and precise in their calculations, and possess a high degree of concentration in order to reduce the risk of error as they assemble prescriptions. They also must be proficient with a variety

A senior care pharmacist administers a flu shot to a patient. *(Jason Sipes, The Altoona Mirror, AP Photo)*

of technical devices and computer systems. In conjunction with these duties, senior care pharmacists need to complete continuing education on a regular basis to maintain their certification or licensing, as required by their states. Continuing education may be done through correspondence (written responses to educational material, usually done online) or by attending conferences, workshops, and seminars. Some states may also require continuing education in particular disease topics and treatments.

REQUIREMENTS

High School

You can start preparing for this career while you are in high school. Begin by taking a college preparatory curriculum. Be sure to take four years of math courses, including algebra, geometry, and trigonometry, and four years of science, including biology, chemistry, and physics. Take computer science classes so that you are comfortable working with computers and English classes to develop your research and writing skills. You may also want to take business classes to learn management skills and business basics. Other courses you should take include history, government, a foreign language, and a social science, such as psychology.

Postsecondary Training

If you want to become a pharmacist, you will need to earn a doctor of pharmacy (known as a Pharm.D. degree). A doctorate degree generally takes six years to complete. The Accreditation Council for Pharmacy Education is the accrediting agency for professional programs in pharmacy.

You will need to complete at least two years of postsecondary study to be accepted to a Pharm.D. program. Most applicants complete three or more years of undergraduate education.

During your undergraduate years, you will complete prepharmacy classes. Studies typically include chemistry, organic chemistry, biology, physics, calculus, statistics, anatomy, English, and social science classes, such as psychology or sociology. After completing this undergraduate work, you will need to gain admission to a school of pharmacy. If you are attending a large university that has a school of pharmacy, you may want to apply there. You may also apply for admission to schools of pharmacy that are not part of your undergraduate school. In addition to completing prepharmacy course work, some pharmacy schools require applicants to take the Pharmacy College Admissions Test (P-CAT) to be considered for admission.

Once you are in pharmacy school, you will take courses such as the principles of pharmacology, biochemistry, pharmacy law and ethics, and pharmaceutical care. Because geriatric pharmacy is a growing field, more and more schools are offering courses with a focus on the elderly and their pharmaceutical care needs. In addition, your education should include an internship, sometimes known as a clerkship, in which you work under the supervision of a professional pharmacist. When deciding on a school to attend, it is advisable that you consult the Accreditation Council for Pharmacy Education's annual *Directory of Accredited Professional Programs of Colleges and Schools of Pharmacy*. Paper copies of this directory are available (at no charge) from the council, and directory information is also available on the council's Web site, http://www.acpe-accredit.org.

Certification or Licensing

The Commission for Certification in Geriatric Pharmacy offers voluntary certification to pharmacists who serve geriatric populations. To become certified, pharmacists must be licensed, have a minimum of two years of experience as a licensed pharmacist, and take a written exam that focuses on geriatric pharmacy practice. Those who pass receive the designation certified geriatric pharmacist. While this is a voluntary certification, professionals in the field highly recommend obtaining it as a demonstration of your specialized skills and knowledge.

All 50 states, the District of Columbia, and U.S. territories require practicing pharmacists to be licensed. To become licensed, candidates must have graduated from an accredited pharmacy program, completed an internship under a licensed pharmacist, and passed their state's board examination.

Other Requirements

Naturally, senior care pharmacists need to be detail-oriented as well as organized. They also need strong communication and people skills since they interact with doctors, nurses, other health professionals, elderly people who are ill, and sometimes an elderly person's family as well. They must be able to work professionally and often patiently when explaining what a medicine will do, how to take it, when to take it, and so on. Senior care pharmacists should also enjoy being around older people and want to help them. These pharmacists must be committed to a lifetime of learning because the fields of medicine and technology continue to grow, making new treatments and new methods of treatment available.

EXPLORING

One way to learn more about this profession is to read publications and visit Web sites dedicated to geriatric pharmacy. (You can start with the organizations' sites listed at the end of this article.) Another option is to get experience in a pharmacy environment by finding part-time or summer work at a drugstore. Even if you aren't working in the pharmacy, you can get valuable experience dealing with customers and observing the kind of work pharmacists do. If you are a hard worker and demonstrate responsibility, you may be given the chance to assist in the pharmacy, such as entering data in customer computer records, taking inventory on pharmaceuticals, bottles, and vials, preparing labels, or making deliveries to customers. Part-time or summer work in a nutrition and vitamin store can also give you the opportunity to learn a great deal about dietary supplements and herbal alternatives to pharmaceuticals.

It is also important that you explore how much you enjoy working with the elderly. Part-time or summer work in a nursing home is one way of doing this. In addition, many volunteer opportunities exist for helping older people. These opportunities can be found with organizations and agencies such as the American Red Cross, states' departments of aging, and local religious agencies, to name a few. You will benefit from getting involved with helping older people, because you will begin to learn about their particular concerns and needs.

EMPLOYERS

Senior care pharmacists traditionally work for nursing home facilities. According to the American Society of Consultant Pharmacists, a number of employers exist within this setting. For example, a senior care pharmacist may work for a small long-term care provider, which provides pharmacy services to several nursing facilities in a small area. A senior care pharmacist can also work for a large long-term care provider, which is a pharmacy providing services to a large number of nursing facilities in a region. A pharmacist in geriatric care can also be hospital-based, working in a hospital's pharmacy and providing services to nursing facilities that are owned or run by the hospital.

There are also a growing number of senior care pharmacists employed in nontraditional settings. These pharmacists may provide services to employers such as assisted living facilities, hospice agencies, and home health programs. In addition, senior care pharmacists may be academically based, teaching at schools of pharmacy; may work in industry for drug companies as administrators or researchers; or may be self-employed, running their own consulting businesses and working with care providers such as nursing facilities, geriatric care managers, and hospice agencies.

The American Society of Consultant Pharmacists, which is the leading organization for those involved in geriatric pharmacy, reports a membership of more than 7,000. While membership is voluntary, this figure gives an idea of the number of pharmacists involved in the field.

STARTING OUT

Those just graduating from pharmacy school should be able to get help locating jobs through their schools' career services offices. Professional organizations are also sources of information; the American Society of Consultant Pharmacists provides a listing of companies that hire recent graduates as well as employment listings on its Web site.

Graduates can also apply to and complete residency programs in geriatric pharmacy. Such a residency will give you further training for working in this field and enhance your credentials. The American Society of Health-System Pharmacists offers several residencies, including residencies in pharmacy practice and residencies in geriatric pharmacy. During a residency, which usually lasts one year, pharmacists work full time and earn a stipend. Residents who complete their programs have excellent employment prospects. Sometimes they are offered jobs at the places of their residencies.

Another option is to begin working in a pharmacy that provides services to a general population, gain work experience, and move into geriatric pharmacy practice when the opportunity presents itself.

ADVANCEMENT

Senior care pharmacists can advance by moving to larger pharmacies for more responsibilities, such as managing a larger staff of pharmacy technicians and working with more nursing facilities than they had in their past jobs. Other senior care pharmacists may consider it an advancement to move into a different area of consulting, for example, changing from nursing facility consulting to long-term care facility consulting. Those in academia advance by becoming full professors, and those in industry may advance by obtaining positions with increased management responsibilities. Some senior care pharmacists with experience may decide to form their own consulting businesses, either alone or in partnership with other pharmacists.

EARNINGS

According to the U.S. Department of Labor, pharmacists had median yearly incomes of $109,180 in 2008. The department also reported that the lowest paid 10 percent earned less than $79,270, while the highest paid 10 percent made more than $134,290 annually.

Some employers view senior care pharmacists as a sort of sales representative in addition to their duties as pharmacists. In these cases, senior care pharmacists are usually at the higher end of the pay scale. Other factors that influence salaries include location and type of employer and the pharmacist's experience.

Pharmacists, in addition to salary, often receive fringe benefits such as paid vacation time, medical and dental insurance, retirement plans, and sometimes bonuses, depending on the size and type of employer.

WORK ENVIRONMENT

Pharmacies must be clean and orderly as well as well lighted and well ventilated. They are frequently busy places and this is especially true for those serving a large number of geriatric patients, since older people often take more than one medication at a time. In addition to working in a pharmacy, senior care pharmacists also visit their patients and consult with other members of the patient's health care team. This means there is a certain amount of travel involved in the senior care pharmacist's work. Additionally, because these pharmacists are in contact with such a variety of people, from elderly people in pain to concerned family members to other health care professionals, they may often need to be diplomatic when advising on why and how medications should be taken.

The two most unfavorable conditions of the pharmacist's practice are the long hours and the necessity to stay on one's feet. Most state laws covering the practice of pharmacy require that there be a pharmacist on duty at all times when a pharmacy is open. This may mean long shifts as, for example, hospital pharmacies are continuously open. Despite these factors, most senior care pharmacists appreciate being involved in health care where they can use their medical and scientific knowledge to help older patients feel better.

Those who run their own businesses have management and financial responsibilities. They must hire employees, keep records on patients, and keep track of costs. They must make rent or mortgage payments and pay insurance premiums and taxes.

OUTLOOK

The U.S. Department of Labor predicts that employment for pharmacists will grow faster than the average for all careers through 2018. The number of available positions is expected to exceed the number of people entering the field, mainly due to pharmacists who are retiring or otherwise leaving the field. Although the U.S. Department of Labor does not provide an employment outlook specifically for senior care pharmacists, it does cite the growing elderly population in the United States as a reason for the good job prospects for pharmacists. Senior citizens are expected to take an increasing number of prescription medications as a result of continuing medical advances and new drug research.

The demand for pharmacists in hospitals will not be as great as other areas of the industry, since hospitals are increasing the amount of outpatient visits and decreasing the length of patient stays; this prompts people to purchase prescriptions from other retail venues, such as drug store and supermarket pharmacies, where job outlooks will be quite good. Other avenues for geriatric pharmacists include working for pharmaceutical manufacturing companies, especially those that manufacture drugs designed to treat ailments that affect senior citizens. In such contexts, pharmacists can work in research and development, or even in the marketing and advertising of new drug products.

FOR MORE INFORMATION

For more information on accredited programs, visit the council's Web site.

Accreditation Council for Pharmacy Education
20 North Clark Street, Suite 2500
Chicago, IL 60602-5109
Tel: 312-664-3575
http://www.acpe-accredit.org

For more information about senior care pharmacists, contact

American Society of Consultant Pharmacists
1321 Duke Street
Alexandria, VA 22314-3563
Tel: 800-355-2727
E-mail: info@ascp.com
http://ascp.com

The society has information on geriatric program residencies and news of interest for those in long-term care.

American Society of Health-System Pharmacists
7272 Wisconsin Avenue
Bethesda, MD 20814-4836
Tel: 301-657-3000
http://www.ashp.org

For information about certification, contact

Speech-Language Pathologists and Audiologists

QUICK FACTS

School Subjects
Biology
Health
Speech

Personal Skills
Helping/teaching
Technical/scientific

Work Environment
Primarily indoors
Primarily one location

Minimum Education Level
Master's degree (speech-language pathologists)
Doctorate (audiologists in some states)

Salary Range
$42,310 to $65,090 to $101,820+ (speech-language pathologists)
$40,650 to $63,230 to $100,480+ (audiologists)

Certification or Licensing
Required by most states (speech-language pathologists)
Required (audiologists)

Outlook
Faster than the average (speech-language pathologists)
Much faster than the average (audiologists)

(continues)

Commission for Certification in Geriatric Pharmacy
1321 Duke Street
Alexandria, VA 22314-3563
Tel: 703-535-3036
E-mail: info@ccgp.org
http://www.ccgp.org

OVERVIEW

Speech-language pathologists and audiologists help people who have speech and hearing defects. They identify the problem, then use tests to further evaluate it. Speech-language pathologists try to improve the speech and language skills of clients with communications disorders. Audiologists perform tests to measure the hearing ability of clients, who may range in age from the very young to the very old. Since it is not uncommon for clients to require assistance in both speech and hearing, pathologists and audiologists may frequently work together to help clients. Some professionals decide to combine these jobs into one, working as *speech-language pathologists/audiologists*. Audiologists and speech-language pathologists may work for school systems, in private practice, and at clinics and other medical facilities. Other employment possibilities for these professionals are teaching, for example, at a universities, and conducting research on what causes certain speech and hearing defects. There are approximately 119,300 speech-language pathologists and 12,800 audiologists employed in the United States.

HISTORY

The diagnosis and treatment of speech and hearing defects is a new part of medical science. In the past, physicians weren't able to help patients with these types of problems because there was usually nothing visibly wrong, and little was known about how speech and hearing were related. Until the middle of the 19th century, medical researchers didn't know whether speech defects were caused by lack of hearing, or whether the patient was the victim of two separate ailments. And even if they could figure out why something was wrong, doctors still couldn't communicate with the patient.

Alexander Graham Bell, the inventor of the telephone, provided some of the answers. His grandfather taught elocution (the art of public speaking), and Bell grew up interested in the problems of speech and hearing. It became his profession, and, by 1871, Bell was lecturing to a class of teachers of deaf people at Boston University. Soon afterward, Bell opened his own school, where he experimented with the idea of making speech visible to his pupils. If he could make them see the movements made by different human tones, they could speak by learning to produce similar vibrations. Bell's efforts not only helped deaf people of his day, but also led directly to the invention of the telephone in 1876. Probably the most famous deaf person was Helen Keller, whose teacher, Anne Sullivan, applied the discoveries of Bell to help Keller overcome her blindness and deafness.

THE JOB

Even though the two professions seem to blend together at times, speech-language pathology and audiology are very different from one another. However, because both speech and hearing are related to one another, a person competent in one discipline must have familiarity with the other.

QUICK FACTS

(continued)

DOT
076

GOE
14.06.01

NOC
3141

O*NET-SOC
29-1127.00 (speech-language pathologists)
29-1121.00 (audiologists)

The duties performed by speech-language pathologists and audiologists differ depending on education and experience and place of employment. Most speech-language pathologists provide direct clinical services to individuals and independently develop and carry out treatment programs. In medical facilities, they may work with physicians, social workers, psychologists, and other therapists to develop and execute treatment plans. In a school environment, they develop individual or group programs, counsel parents, and sometimes help teachers with classroom activities.

Clients of speech-language pathologists include people who cannot make speech sounds, or cannot make them clearly; those with speech rhythm and fluency problems such as stuttering; people with voice quality problems, such as inappropriate pitch or harsh voice; those with problems understanding and producing language; and those with cognitive communication impairments, such as attention, memory, and problem-solving disorders. Speech-language pathologists may also work with people who have oral motor problems that cause eating and swallowing difficulties. Clients' problems may be congenital, developmental, or acquired and caused by hearing loss, brain injury or deterioration, cerebral palsy, stroke, cleft palate, voice pathology, mental retardation, or emotional problems.

Speech-language pathologists conduct written and oral tests and use special instruments to analyze and diagnose the nature and extent of impairment. They develop an individualized plan of care, which may include automated devices and sign language. They teach clients how to make sounds, improve their voices, or increase their language skills to communicate more effectively. Speech-language pathologists help clients develop, or recover, reliable communication skills.

People who have hearing, balance, and related problems consult audiologists, who use audiometers and other testing devices to discover the nature and extent of hearing loss. Audiologists interpret these results and may coordinate them with medical, educational, and psychological information to make a diagnosis and determine a course of treatment.

Hearing disorders can result from trauma at birth, viral infections, genetic disorders, exposure to loud noise, or simply old age. Treatment may include examining and cleaning the ear canal, fitting and dispensing a hearing aid or other device, and audiologic rehabilitation (including auditory training or instruction in speech or lip reading). Audiologists provide fitting and tuning of cochlear implants and help those with implants adjust to the implant amplification systems. They also test noise levels in workplaces and conduct hearing protection programs in industry, as well as in schools and communities.

Audiologists provide direct clinical services to clients and sometimes develop and implement individual treatment programs. In some environments, however, they work as members of professional teams in planning and implementing treatment plans.

In a research environment, speech pathologists and audiologists investigate communicative disorders and their causes and ways to improve clinical services. Those teaching in colleges and universities instruct students on the principles and bases of communication, communication disorders, and clinical techniques used in speech and hearing.

Speech-language pathologists and audiologists keep records on the initial evaluation, progress, and discharge of clients to identify problems and track progress. They counsel individuals and their families on how to cope with the stress and misunderstanding that often accompany communication disorders.

REQUIREMENTS

High School

Since a college degree is a must for practicing this profession, make sure your high school classes are geared toward preparing you for higher education. Health and science classes, including biology, are important to take. Mathematics classes and English classes will help you develop research, writing, and math skills that you will need in college. Because speech pathologists and audiologists work so intensely with language, you may also find it beneficial to study a foreign language, paying special attention to how you learn to make sounds and remember words. Speech classes will also improve your awareness of sounds and language as well as improve your speaking and listening skills.

Postsecondary Training

Most states require a master's degree in speech-language pathology or audiology for a beginning job in either profession. Forty-seven states required speech-language pathologists to be licensed if they work in a health care setting, and 12 states require the same license to practice in a public school. Typical majors for those going into this field include communication sciences and disorders, speech and hearing, or education. Regardless of your career goal (speech-language pathologist or audiologist), your undergraduate course work should include classes in anatomy, biology, physiology, physics, and other related areas, such as linguistics, semantics, and phonetics. If you plan to specialize in working with the elderly, you should consider earning a degree in gerontology.

To be eligible for certification, which most employers and states require, you must have at least a master's degree from a program accredited by the accreditation council of the American Speech-Language-Hearing Association (ASHA). Currently there are more than 300 programs in speech-language pathology and/or audiology; however, not all of these programs are accredited. It is in your best interest to contact the ASHA for a listing of accredited programs before you decide on a graduate school to attend. Accredited graduate programs in speech-language pathology are available from approximately 240 colleges and universities. Currently, 18 states require that audiologists earn a doctorate for certification, and according to the ASHA, as of 2012, audiologists will have to earn a doctorate in order to be certified. There are more than 70 accredited doctoral programs in audiology.

Some schools offer graduate degrees only in speech-language pathology or graduate degrees only in audiology. A number of schools offer degrees in both fields. Graduate-level course work in audiology includes such studies as hearing and language disorders, normal auditory and speech-language development, balance, and audiology instrumentation. Graduate-level work for those in speech-language pathologist includes studies in evaluating and treating speech and language disorders, stuttering, pronunciation, and voice modulation. Students of both disciplines are required to complete supervised clinical fieldwork or practicum.

If you plan to go into research, teaching, or administration, you will need to complete a doctorate degree.

Certification or Licensing

To work as a speech pathologist or audiologist in a public school, you will be required to be a certified teacher and you must meet special state requirements if treating children with disabilities. Almost all states regulate audiology and/or speech-language pathology through licensure or title registration, and all but six of those require continuing education for license renewal. In order to become licensed, you must have completed an advanced degree in the field (generally a master's degree, but a doctorate is becoming standard for audiologists), pass a standardized test, and complete 300 to 375 hours of supervised clinical experience and nine months of postgraduate professional clinical experience. Some states permit audiologists to dispense hearing aids under an audiology license. Specific education and experience requirements, type of regulation, and title use vary by state.

Many states base their licensing laws on ASHA certification. ASHA offers speech-language pathologists the certificate of clinical competence in speech-language pathology and audiologists the cer-

An audiologist uses an otoscope to conduct a hearing screening at a community health fair. *(Peter Hvizdak, The Image Works)*

tificate of clinical competence in audiology. To be eligible for these certifications, you must meet certain education requirements, such as the supervised clinical fieldwork experience, and have completed a postgraduate clinical fellowship. The fellowship must be no less than 36 weeks of full-time professional employment or its part-time equivalent. You must then pass an examination in the area in which you want certification.

Other Requirements

Naturally, speech-language pathologists and audiologists should have strong communication skills. Note, though, that this means more than being able to speak clearly. You must be able to explain diagnostic test results and treatment plans in an easily understood way for a variety of clients who are already experiencing problems. As a speech-language pathologist and audiologist, you should enjoy working with people, both your clients and other professionals who may be involved in the client's treatment. In addition, you need patience and compassion. A client's progress may be slow, and you should be supportive and encouraging during these times. If you plan on working with the elderly, you should remember that some speech and hearing problems may not be able to be completely cured as a result of a medical condition (such as damage caused by a stroke). In these instances, it is important to maintain a positive attitude and try to help the patient recover as much of his or her former capacities as possible.

EXPLORING

Although the specialized nature of this work makes it difficult for you to get an informal introduction to either profession, there are opportunities to be found. Official training must begin at the college or university level, but it is possible for you to volunteer in clinics and hospitals. As a prospective speech-language pathologist and audiologist, you may also find it helpful to learn sign language or volunteer your time in speech, language, and hearing centers. If you would like to work with the elderly, any experience you can gain interacting with senior citizens will be useful.

EMPLOYERS

There are approximately 119,300 speech-language pathologists and 12,800 audiologists employed in the United States. About 48 percent of speech-language pathologists are employed in education, from elementary school to the university level. About 64 percent of audiologists work in physicians' offices and medical facilities. Other professionals in this field work in state and local governments, hearing aid stores (audiologists), and scientific research facilities. A small but growing number of speech-language pathologists and audiologists are in private practice, generally working with patients referred to them by physicians and other health practitioners.

Some speech-language pathologists and audiologists contract to provide services in schools, hospitals, or nursing homes, or work as consultants to industry. Audiologists are more likely to be employed in independent health care offices, while speech-language pathologists are more likely to work in school settings.

STARTING OUT

If you want to work in the public school systems, your college career services office can help you with interviewing skills. Professors sometimes know of job openings and may even post these openings on a centrally located bulletin board. It may be possible to find employment by contacting a hospital or rehabilitation center. To work in colleges and universities as a specialist in the classroom, clinic, or research center, it is almost mandatory to be working on a graduate degree. Many scholarships, fellowships, and grants for assistants are available in colleges and universities giving courses in speech-language pathology and audiology. Most of these and other assistance programs are offered at the graduate level. The Rehabilitation Services Administration, the Children's Bureau of the Administration for Children and Families, the U.S. Department of Education, and the National Institutes of Health allocate funds for teaching and training grants to colleges and universities with graduate study programs. In addition, the U.S. Department of Veterans Affairs provides stipends (a fixed allowance) for predoctoral work.

ADVANCEMENT

Advancement in speech-language pathology and audiology is based chiefly on education. Individuals who have completed graduate study will have the best opportunities to enter research and administrative areas, supervising other speech-language pathologists or audiologists either in developmental work or in public school systems.

EARNINGS

The U.S. Department of Labor (DOL) reports that speech-language pathologists earned a median annual salary of $65,090 in 2009. Salaries ranged from to less than $42,310 to more than $101,820. The DOL reports the following mean annual salaries for speech-language pathologists by employer: home health care services, $87,820; nursing care facilities, $80,500; community care facilities for the elderly, $79,130; and general medical and surgical hospitals, $72,030. Also in 2009, audiologists earned a median annual salary of $63,230. The lowest paid 10 percent of these workers earned less than $40,650, while the highest paid 10 percent earned $100,480 or more per year. Geographic location and type of facility are important salary variables. Almost all employment situations provide fringe benefits such as paid vacations, sick leave, and retirement programs. Self-employed speech-language pathologists and audiologists must provide their own benefits.

WORK ENVIRONMENT

Most speech-language pathologists and audiologists work 40 hours a week at a desk or table in clean comfortable surroundings. Speech-language pathologists and audiologists who focus on research, however, may work longer hours. The job is not physically demanding but does require attention to detail and intense concentration. The emotional needs of clients and their families may be demanding.

OUTLOOK

Population growth, lengthening life spans, and increased public awareness of the problems associated with communicative disorders indicate a highly favorable employment outlook for well-qualified personnel. The U.S. Department of Labor predicts that employment for speech-language pathologists and audiologists will grow faster and much faster than the average, respectively, for all occupations through 2018. Much of this growth depends on economic factors, further budget cutbacks by health care providers and third-party payers, and legal mandates requiring services for people with disabilities.

Nearly half of the new jobs emerging through the end of the decade are expected to be in speech and hearing clinics, physicians' offices, and outpatient care facilities. Speech-language pathologists and audiologists will be needed in these places, for example, to carry out the increasing number of rehabilitation programs for stroke victims and patients with head injuries.

Substantial job growth will continue to occur in elementary and secondary schools because of the Education for All Handicapped Children Act of 1975 (which was renamed the Individuals with Disabilities Education Act and amended in 1990, 1997, and 2004). This law guarantees special education and related services to minors with disabilities.

Many new jobs will be created in hospitals, nursing homes, rehabilitation centers, and home health agencies; most of these openings will probably be filled by private practitioners employed on a contract basis. Opportunities for speech-language pathologists and audiologists in private practice should increase in the future. There should be a greater demand for consultant audiologists in the area of industrial and environmental noise as manufacturing and other companies develop and carry out noise-control programs. Speech-language pathologists and audiologists who are fluent in a foreign language (such as Spanish) should have especially strong employment prospects.

FOR MORE INFORMATION

The American Auditory Society is concerned with hearing disorders, how to prevent them, and the rehabilitation of individuals with hearing and balance dysfunction.
American Auditory Society
19 Mantua Road
Mt. Royal, NJ 08061-1006

Tel: 856-423-3118
http://www.amauditorysoc.org

This professional, scientific, and credentialing association offers information about communication disorders and career information.

American Speech-Language-Hearing Association
2200 Research Boulevard
Rockville, MD 20850-3289
Tel: 800-638-8255
E-mail: actioncenter@asha.org
http://www.asha.org

This association is for undergraduate and graduate students studying human communication. For information on accredited training programs, news related to the field, and to find out about regional chapters, contact

National Student Speech Language Hearing Association
2200 Research Boulevard, Suite 450
Rockville, MD 20850-3289
E-mail: nsslha@asha.org
http://www.nsslha.org

Index

Index